BOUNDARY WATERS

CANOE CAMPING

CLIFF JACOBSON

Illustrated by Cliff Moen

For Mark
Merry Christmas
2001
from Mom + Brent
Hopefully you will make more
trips to the BWCA and someday
take Ben + Laurii!

The Globe Pequot Press

Guilford, Connecticut

DEDICATION

To John Baumann
A kind and gentle man whose dreams took him
beyond the beaten path.

Cover design: Adam Schwartzman
Cover photos: © Bob Firth
Text design: Lisa Reneson
Illustrations: Cliff Moen

Library of Congress Cataloging-in-Publication Data
Jacobson, Cliff.
   Boundary waters canoe camping/Cliff Jacobson; illustrated by Cliff Moen.—2nd ed.
      p.   cm.
   Rev. ed. of: Boundary waters. 1995.
   ISBN 0-7627-0667-8
      1. Canoe camping—Minnesota—Boundary Waters Canoe Area—Guidebooks. 2. Canoes and canoeing—Minnesota—Boundary Waters Canoe Area—Guidebooks. 3. Boundary Waters Canoe Area (Minn.)—Guidebooks. I. Jacobson, Cliff. Boundary waters. II. Title.
GV790.J32   2000
796.54'09776'7—dc21   00-020128

Manufactured in the United States of America
Second Edition/Second Printing

Contents

A Note to the Reader

Preface, by Kevin Proescholdt

Chapter 1 A Wilderness in Turmoil, by David Backes, 1

Chapter 2 Planning and Pacing Your Canoe Trip, 7

First, Pick Your Travel Area 8
Maps 11
If You Plan To Use a GPS 12
Don't Turn Your Vacation into a Marathon! 13
Rules for Interpreting Contour Lines 15
Planning the Route 17
Scenario Thought List 17
Permits 18

Chapter 3 A Maze of Finger Lakes, Portage Trails, and Confusing Bays!, 23

Maps 24
Orienteering Compass 24
No Need to Worry about Magnetic Declination! .24
Using Map and Compass Together 25
Test Your Map and Compass Skills 28
Aiming Off 28
Tips for Navigating Small Streams and Moose Trails 29

Chapter 4 Favorite Routes—Where Solitude Still Remains, 31

Ham Lake to Long Island Lake and Points East 31
Frost River 33
Granite River through Guide's Portage 35

Chapter 5 Federal Regulations and Rational, 39

Quotas 40
Some Obscure Regulations 41
No Cans or Bottles Are Allowed in the BWCA! 41

Camouflage Your Camp 41
Camp Only at U.S. Forest Service Designated Sites 42
When Nature Calls and There Is No Forest Service Box Latrine 42
Campfires Are Allowed Only Within the Steel Fire
   Grates at Developed Campsites 43
Sanitation and Waste Disposal 44

Chapter 6 Selecting and Outfitting Your Canoe, 47

A Boundary Waters Canoe Can Never Be Too Light! 47
A Fast Canoe Is a Welcome Luxury 47
Canoe Building Materials 48
Canoe Tips 48
Outfitting the Canoe 49

Chapter 7 Paddling and Portaging Your Canoe, 55

Paddling Your Canoe 55
Big Water Tactics 59
Portaging Your Canoe 66

Chapter 8 The Right Stuff—Everything You Need To Know about Equipment, 71

Packs 72
Tent 78
Cooking Tarp 78
Stove 79
Edged Tools 80
Clothing 80
Rain Gear 80
Hats 81
Footwear 81
Sleeping Gear 82
Kids' Stuff 82
Packing Your Packs 84
Packing the Canoe 85

Chapter 9 Fast Fixin's—Easy Ways to Prepare Great Trail Meals, 87

Hardware 88
Spices 90

Packing the Kitchen 90
Containers for Powders and Liquids 90
Easy Breakfasts 90
Launching Lunch 92
On into Supper 93
Meal Management Tricks 95
Tasty Cooking Tricks 97

Chapter 10 A Bomb-Proof Canoe Camp!, 101

Tents and Tarps 102
Campfires 104

Chapter 11 Bothersome Beasts and Ornery Stingers!, 109

Bothersome Beasts 109
Ornery Stingers 114

Chapter 12 Dangers, Safety, and First Aid, 121

Swimming Don'ts! 121
Lightning 122
Widow-Makers 124
When Your Canoe Becomes a Kite! 124
Safety with Edged Tools 125
Water Quality 125
Medicine for the Boundary Waters 127
First Aid for Common Ailments 129
Signals: When You Need To Bring the Airplane Down! 131

Chapter 13 A Magic Day in the BWCA, 133

Chapter 14 Advice from the Experts, 137

Allen Todnem 137
Neil Bernstein 138
Ken E. Brown 138
Tom and Sue Chelstrom 139
Dr. Nick Boismenue and Stephanie Urbonya 140
Barry Tungseth 140

Sue Harings 141
Jeff Destross 142
Jim Dale Huot-Vickery 143
Advice from an Outfitter—Marti and Bob Marchino 143

Appendix 1 Equipment Checklist, 145

Appendix 2 Resources, 149

BWCA Information and Permits 149
Quetico Information and Permits 150
Customs 150
Minnesota Licenses 150
Organizations 151
Information on Resorts and Outfitters 151
Maps 152
Miscellaneous Equipment and Supplies 152
Packsacks, Map Cases, and Other Canoeing Luggage 154
BWCA and Quetico Canoeing Guide Books 155

Appendix 3 Seven-Day Menu, 156

Appendix 4 The Wilderness Meal, 159

Appendix 5 McKenzie Map Index, 165

Index, 169

A Note to the Reader

What? Another book on canoeing the Boundary Waters? That was my reaction when friends prodded me to write this book. However, as my thoughts began to meld, I realized that my background as a Boundary Waters guide and Canadian river expedition leader could shed new light on traditional ways.

For example, lightweight camping equipment has simplified the BWCA experience, though some traditional products, like Duluth packs, Minnesota-style canoe yokes, wool shirts, and L. L. Bean boots continue to defy the competition.

Thankfully, campfires are still permitted in the Boundary Waters, though most modern voyageurs prefer to cook on single-burner trail stoves. However, special techniques are required to prevent thick soups and cereals from burning in the intense heat of a gas stove. I'll share these expedition tricks with you in Chapter 9, along with my most popular recipes, like pita pizza and steamed cinnamon-sugar tortillas. You'll also learn how to use pot insulators and cozies to save stove fuel and keep foods hot.

In Chapters 2 and 4, you'll discover that you don't have to make tough portages to get away from the crowd! In Chapter 10, there are serious skills for maintaining command when the weather turns sour. Chapter 12 details safety concerns and hazards that are unique to this land of proud granite. If you'll be tripping in June when the insects are bad, you may want to avoid dark blue clothing and construct the "Susie bug net" described in Chapter 11. If you're canoeing with kids, you'll want to read the field-proven advice in Chapter 8. And in Chapter 14, you'll find some expert tips that will smooth your Boundary Waters experience.

In time, you'll relish the challenge that comes with rain, wind, waves, and unfamiliar routes. As you gain experience, you'll realize that knowledge—not expensive gear—is what's most needed to make an enjoyable trip through the Boundary Waters. Most of all, I hope you'll gain an appreciation for the fragile nature of the Boundary Waters Canoe Area and a deep respect for the men and women who have fought—and continue to fight—to preserve its wild heritage. New federal regulations (you'll read all about them in Chapter 5) and a better visitor distribution program ensure that the wildness of this region will remain intact for future generations to enjoy.

Cliff Jacobson

Help Us Keep This Guide Up to Date

Every effort has been made by the author and editors to make this guide as accurate and useful as possible. However, many things can change after a guide is published—new products and information become available, regulations change, techniques evolve, etc.

We would love to hear from you concerning your experiences with this guide and how you feel it could be improved and be kept up to date. While we may not be able to respond to all comments and suggestions, we'll take them to heart and we'll also make certain to share them with the author. Please send your comments and suggestions to the following address:

The Globe Pequot Press
Reader Response/Editorial Department
P.O. Box 480
Guilford, CT 06437

Or you may e-mail us at:

editorial@globe-pequot.com

Thanks for your input, and happy travels!

Preface

The Boundary Waters Canoe Area is a hauntingly beautiful place—a million acres of glacier-scoured bedrock covered with birch and pine forests, laced with over a thousand sparkling lakes. Rivers and streams, or portage trails through the woods, connect these lakes along and just south of the international border between Minnesota and Ontario. Cliffs plunge deep into lakes here, rivers tumble over waterfalls and through rapids, and loons yodel their eerie calls across moonlit lakes. An original unit of the national Wilderness Preservation System, the Boundary Waters Canoe Area is the largest wilderness east of the Rockies and north of Florida's Everglades. This unique region contains the largest block of virgin forest in the eastern United States and provides home to a host of native wild species like moose, otters, bald eagles, and the rare eastern timber wolf.

The BWCA is also an integral part of an international wilderness complex known as the Quetico-Superior Ecosystem. This broader region includes Ontario's 1.2 million-acre Quetico Provincial Park, the 219,000-acre Voyageurs National Park just west of the Boundary Waters, and other key lands. Altogether, the Quetico-Superior Ecosystem is an internationally significant treasure of some 2.5 million acres!

The Boundary Waters area has not always enjoyed wilderness protection. We are the recipients of a storied legacy that began in the early part of this century. Through the efforts of wilderness advocates like Sigurd Olson, Ernest Oberholtzer, Bob Marshall, Bud Heinselman, and thousands of others, the BWCA remains free from resource and recreational development. But preserving the wildness of this wilderness requires unrelenting vigilance.

Surprisingly, the world's most famous canoe country is at risk from those of us who come to explore its waterways and seek its charms. Because of its beauty and allure, the Boundary Waters Canoe Area is the most heavily visited wilderness in the nation. An estimated 200,000 people annually accumulate 1.5 million "recreation visitor days" of use in the Boundary

Waters. Unless we ensure that adequate protections are in place, we threaten to love the area to death, damaging campsites and destroying the very solitude and silence we seek.

All of us who visit the canoe country must remember that the wilderness was there first, that the area and its wildlife have immense "biocentric" values beyond just recreation. We must learn to leave no trace of our passing, and to practice minimum-impact camping techniques. We must remain alert for practices that would threaten the wildness of the Boundary Waters and willingly embrace environmental organizations that press for protective policies. If we care enough about the Boundary Waters, we can pass on a priceless legacy of protected wilderness to our heirs.

Kevin Proescholdt
Director, Friends of the Boundary Waters Wilderness

A Wilderness in Turmoil
by David Backes

In June 1921, a twenty-two-year-old high school teacher from Nashwauk, Minnesota, made his first canoe trip into the Boundary Waters, and recorded observations in a pocket notebook. "This is beautiful," he wrote one afternoon while windbound on a rocky island in Seagull Lake. "Everything is as God made it, untouched by man. My dreams have come true. I've seen real wild country and have not been disappointed."

He almost died before the trip began, barely avoiding a plunge over a water- fall, and his notebook describes mosquito-ridden nights, painful portaging, and two times when his group was lost for hours, but Sigurd Olson was hooked. Within two years he moved to Ely, Minnesota, right at the edge of the Boundary Waters, and began developing his long relationship with wilderness that eventual- ly bore fruit in widely read books of nature essays and in his work as a leader in the struggle to save the last great remnants of North American wilderness. Through it all, he fought longest and hardest to make it possible for future gener- ations to experience genuine wilderness in the Boundary Waters he had loved since 1921.

While few achieve the kind of recognition enjoyed by a Sigurd Olson, many have followed the same basic pattern: The canoe country steals their hearts and eventually their time.

Call it a paradox. There's something about this rugged land that fills people with peace and makes them ready to do battle.

And there have been plenty of battles over the Boundary Waters, involving more court hearings and pieces of legislation than probably any other wilderness area in North America. I don't know of another wilderness, for example, that has been raided by the FBI.

You haven't heard that story? It happened in 1953, four years after President Harry Truman had signed a precedent-setting executive order forbidding airplanes from flying into the Boundary Waters. The owners of three resorts on Crooked Lake and Lac la Croix had challenged the order in federal court and lost. They planned on appealing to the U.S. Supreme Court (the court ultimately refused to hear the case), but meanwhile they defied a federal appeals court injunction and continued to fly in up to 200 people a day.

On June 30, 1953, three FBI agents and two U.S. marshals joined forest rangers and game wardens in Ely and planned the operation. On July 2 the U.S. marshals flew to the resorts, seized the planes, arrested the pilots, and handed subpoenas to the resort owners. Over the next several days Forest Service officials flew stranded resort guests back to Ely, where they were questioned by the FBI agents and had their fishing licenses checked by the game wardens. The New York Times ran stories three days in a row, with such titles as "Campers Stranded as U.S. Seizes Planes Violating Ban in Minnesota" and "Two Hundred in Woods Face Rough Trip Home."

It sounds funny now, but it was deadly earnest at the time. The airplane controversy was among the most bitter in the canoe country's history. In Ely it turned some families inside out. Neighbors wouldn't speak to each other. People who attended the same church would turn away from each other.

The city's establishment was decidedly pro-airplane, so it was especially tough for those who favored banning planes from the wilderness. The Ely *Miner* published flagrant lies about airplane opponents. Sigurd Olson, for example, returned from a canoe trip in August 1948 to find himself accused of owning stock in timber companies and trying to ban airplanes so the loggers could clear-cut the interior portions of the wilderness without being seen. In the charged atmosphere people actually believed it.

Another Miner story, equally false, sparked death threats against Frank Hubachek, a leading proponent of the airplane ban. Then there was the owner of Ely's radio station, who sold the station shortly after broadcasting a story about fishermen illegally flying fish out of the wilderness; he said he couldn't take the threats anymore. And a small bomb was detonated in the backyard of Bill Rom, an outfitter who favored the ban.

I often think of the courage of those people in Ely and Winton and Tower and other northeastern Minnesota communities who stood up for their belief in preserving the wilderness canoe country despite the harassment they knew they would endure. Sigurd Olson was not the only one who was told he would lose his job if he kept up his wilderness activism; he's just the best known. And eventually his fame protected him from most kinds of abuse, at least if you don't count his being hanged in effigy at the age of 78.

At times the same kind of courage has been required of canoe country defenders outside of northeastern Minnesota. I think especially of a battle against waterpower development in the late 1920s and early 1930s. Edward W. Backus, one of the last of the timber barons, wanted to build a series of storage dams, and eight of them were to be built smack in the middle of the canoe country. The dams would have generated 20,000 horsepower for his power dams between Rainy Lake and Lake Winnipeg. They also would have raised lake levels as high as eighty feet in places, flooding thousands of miles of shoreline. Basswood Falls, Curtain Falls, Rebecca and Birch Falls would have been wiped out. Lac la Croix would have lost nearly all of its 300 islands.

A group of brave men, however, formed an organization called the Quetico-Superior Council to fight Backus. Rallying behind a proposal for an international wilderness reserve that was drafted by an energetic and visionary man named Ernest Oberholtzer, the Council put Backus on the defensive and ultimately out-lasted him. But it wasn't easy on the activists, many of them from Minneapolis and Chicago. Backus pulled out all the stops, getting banks to call back notes of those who opposed his plan, and using contacts to put pressure on them in the workplace.

Fighting Boundary Waters battles hasn't always required heroism, however. Every fight has had its heroes, but every fight has depended in the end on the just plain hard work of average people who love the wilderness. Rarely do they get any publicity, just the satisfaction of contributing to a cause in which they deeply believe.

Frank Robertson, of Minnesota's Mesabi Range country, was the epitome of these foot soldiers. Not especially articulate, not one to give lengthy speeches or write articles or lobby legislators, he played a key role in the fight to ban airplanes from the wilderness. He took a documentary film about the issue from town to town all over northeastern Minnesota, showing it to any civic group that would let him in: Rotary clubs, garden clubs, American Legions, church groups, chambers of commerce. Over the course of a couple of years' worth of weekends and weekday evenings he showed the film more than 800 times, wearing out his first copy after 500 showings.

Because of Frank Robertson's efforts more than seventy-five organizations passed resolutions in favor of the airplane ban. This provided empirical evidence to counter the claims of airplane supporters that local opinion was solidly behind them, and made it easier for the newly elected Senator Hubert Humphrey and for Representative John Blatnik to risk siding with the preservationists. If they had opposed the ban, President Truman would not have signed the executive order.

There have been too many other battles to describe in this short space—battles over logging and outboard motors and snowmobiles, for example—but they always have addressed the same basic question: What kind of place should the Boundary Waters be? If it is meant to provide people not just with clean air, physical adventure, and mouth-watering walleyed pike, but also with experiences of solitude and silence and a sense of kinship with the natural world from which they come, then the answer is clear: This is no place for logging or motors, and the number of visitors must be carefully managed.

If this is your answer, be prepared to defend it, for to carry out such convictions inevitably means hurting the interests of a number of other people, most of whom live near the canoe country. It's easy to stereotype resort owners and loggers as greedy, and to portray other area residents who oppose further restrictions as narrow-minded and selfish, but in fact they're just like everyone else. They've got children to feed and clothe, mortgages to pay, health insurance to purchase, and retirement savings to worry about. The difference is that they live next to this beautiful wilderness, and depend on the canoe country either for their living or for their primary recreations. Compared to people living in large cities, they have fewer options to fall back upon when their livelihood is threatened.

Also, realize that northeastern Minnesotans have never enjoyed much control over their economy. The big logging companies came and went, and so did most of the mining companies. Local people never controlled these companies; their jobs were at the whims of people who lived far away. Tourism has been the most significant locally controlled industry this part of the state has ever had; no wonder area residents often react heatedly to proposed wilderness regulations.

Those of us who want to keep the Boundary Waters wild have a double task, then: to be vigilant for threats to the tangible and intangible qualities that make the canoe country precious, and to do so in a way that does not place an unjust burden on the people who live nearby. Anything that we can do to promote a healthy and environmentally sound local economy will reap wilderness benefits.

Finding some sort of common ground, or at least building mutual respect, between non-local preservationists and area residents will become increasingly important over the next half century because the Great Lakes region is likely to improve its industrial base. The West is running out of water, but the Midwest has it in abundance. A large increase in the region's population will certainly mean a large increase in potential visitors to the Boundary Waters. There quite likely will be pressure to relax the daily limits on the number of people who can enter the wilderness. Preservationists will find it easier to defend visitor restrictions if they can work with area residents to attract tourist traffic to the lakes and woods outside of the wilderness.

Yes, there will be battles ahead. That is a given. But as long as there are people who not only love the wilderness but are willing to give of themselves to defend it, there is hope. The next time you visit the Boundary Waters, remember that. And when you find yourself at peace some evening as the sun casts its last quivering rays over the water and a loon gives out a long, mournful cry—when it finally hits you just how quiet it is—remember how that solitude and silence were bought for you by the sweat and dedication of hundreds of people over many years. Remember them. Enjoy the spirit of the wild. And vow to defend it.

David Backes holds a Ph.D. in environmental communication from the University of Wisconsin–Madison and is a professor in the Department of Journalism and Mass Communication at UW–Milwaukee. He fell in love with the Boundary Waters in 1963, when his family first visited the area. Mr. Backes has authored three powerful books, which I commend to your attention. *Canoe Country: An Embattled Wilderness* (NorthWord Press, 1991) is a lively history of the Boundary Waters that has received international praise. *The Wilderness Companion* (NorthWord Press, 1992) is a thought-provoking collection of memorable quotes from a variety of respected sources. *A Wilderness Within* (University of Minnesota Press, 1997) is the life story of wilderness giant Sigurd F. Olson.

Planning and Pacing Your Canoe Trip

I grew up in southern Indiana where a two-acre farm pond qualifies as a lake. So imagine my chagrin when I got my first view of the Boundary Waters from a sandy rise above Saganaga Lake. Ten miles long and half as wide, Saganaga had hundreds of islands, bays, and channels to confuse the route our Grand Marais outfitter had outlined on our map. And beyond the wind-protected shoreline there were whitecaps—big ones! I searched the lake for sign of a canoe. There was none.

My partner and I exchanged worried glances and then burst out laughing. Back home in Indiana we were pros; here in Minnesota we were *Cheechakos* in a foreign land. Canoe this heaving lake today? No way!

After a short discussion, we decided to reverse our proposed route and begin our trip on nearby Seagull Lake. Seagull was about half the size of Saganaga and it had more islands to break the wind. We figured that once we reached Miles Island, we could follow the lee shore all the way to the first portage.

We encountered breaking waves as soon as we cleared the channel and headed west onto the big lake. Eyes glued to our maps, we threaded our way through a maze of wind-protected islands. Thirty minutes later, we identified the small, rock-walled harbor of Miles Island, where we paused to reflect on the fate of other canoeists who might not be so proficient in map and compass work.

"I'll bet a lot of people spend a lot of time paddling around wondering where they're at," mused my friend, John Orr.

A moment later, we spotted three canoes paddling slowly toward us. When they were within hailing distance, a man called out, "You guys know where we are?"

"Miles Island," I yelled proudly. The man waved his thanks and the canoes went on their way.

Contrary to popular belief, experienced canoeists *do* get lost in the Boundary Waters, though usually not for very long. Veteran paddlers know that new routes breed new challenges. Probing an unfamiliar stream to its hidden source, finding an obscure portage or bay—such adventures are all part of the Boundary Waters experience. Wondering what's around the next bend adds adventure to what might otherwise be a bland vacation.

If you want to see the Boundary Waters in a fresh new light on every trip you take, you must accept the uneasiness (call it mild fear, if you will) that often accompanies breaking new ground. However, until you've earned your wings, you'll want to keep challenges small, short, and manageable. It takes years to develop good judgment and proficient outdoor skills. You can't rush time.

Let's put things into perspective with this scenario. Four of you—all good friends—are planning a canoe trip into the Boundary Waters. Figure on seven days of midsummer fun and adventure. The crew wants an interesting and diverse route—one with beaver ponds, streams, small rapids, manageable lakes, and picturesque waterfalls. A few tough portages are okay, as long as they're not too long. Relative isolation is a must. Paddling days should be short—five hours at most—and there should be at least one layover day on which everyone can just hang around. Here's how to realize your dream.

First, Pick Your Travel Area

Contact the Superior National Forest and request a free Boundary Waters Canoe Area Wilderness travel pack:

> Superior National Forest
> 8901 Grand Avenue Place
> Duluth, MN 55808-1102
> Phone: (218) 626–4300
> TDD: (218) 626–4399
> Web site: www.fs.fed.us/r9/superior

You'll receive an abbreviated map and list of Boundary Waters Canoe Area (BWCA) entry points (**Figure 2-1**), permit and fee information, rules and regulations, and the names and addresses of Forest Service Ranger stations and tourist associations that service the BWCA. Specific questions about an area or route (water levels, difficulty of portages, and so forth) should be directed to the Ranger district that services that route. Appendix 2 contains the most important U.S. and Canadian addresses.

For planning purposes, the Boundary Waters can be broken into four zones, each of which presents different challenges.

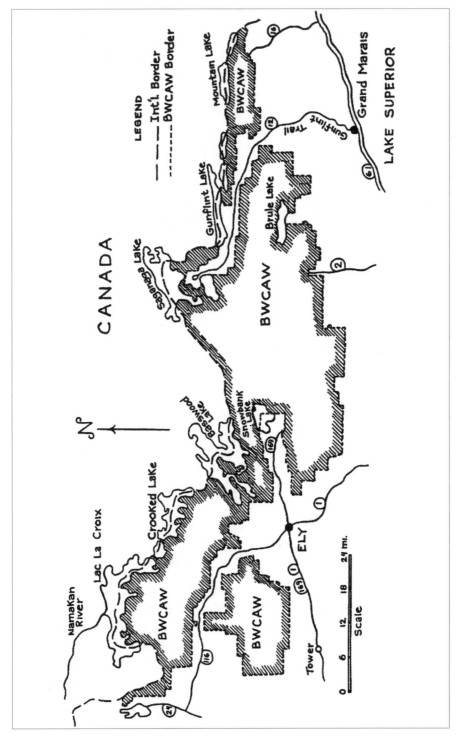

Figure 2-1

The northwestern edge of the BWCA, called the Cook Area, is characterized by huge lakes like Trout, Crane, and Vermillion. The Namakan River, which originates at sprawling Lac la Croix and terminates on the edge of Voyageur's National Park, is a classic whitewater route for experienced paddlers who like big rapids. Of course, there are more intimate routes, like the Nina Moose and Little Indian Sioux Rivers, but basically this is big lake country—better suited to motor boats than canoes. On the whole, beginners will find better canoeing farther east.

Ely

Once a strong mining town, Ely now caters largely to the canoeing crowd. Attractions include the International Wolf Center, Vermillion Interpretive and History Museum (it's great!), and the world-renowned Soudan underground mine. A number of commercial outfitters offer state-of-the-art gear at very reasonable prices.

The area around Ely has routes for every skill level. The more popular lakes—Moose, Basswood, Snowbank, and Lakes One, Two, Three, and Four—are fairly large and complex, and are very heavily traveled. There are smaller waters, though accessing them often means starting your trip on big water or making some tough portages. Exceptions include the wind-sheltered Kawishiwi and Isabella Rivers, which lie off Highway 1.

Tofte/Isabella

Twenty-five miles southwest of Grand Marais, on Highway 61, is the rustic Tofte Ranger Station, which stands sentry to the famed Sawbill Trail.

Most Sawbill-area lakes are small and easy to navigate. Portages are well maintained, reasonably short, and easy to find. And the scenery is among the best in the Boundary Waters. For example, Brule and Cherokee Lakes are renowned for their high cliffs, rugged shorelines and beautiful overlooks. Cherokee Creek, which is maintained by a large beaver colony, silently winds through a mile of prime moose habitat.

Grand Marais

This is my favorite jumping-off place. Part of the allure is the town itself, which overlooks Lake Superior. There are a harbor, a lighthouse, and several tourist shops and restaurants, plus the East Bay Hotel, a renovated turn-of-the-century establishment. Joyne's General Store contains everything from socks and popcorn to long underwear and frying pans. The Superior North Shore drive is one of the most beautiful in the world.

The Gunflint Trail heads north out of Grand Marais and accesses some of the most diverse canoe country in the Boundary Waters. In Chapter 4, I've outlined some of my favorite routes originating in this area. Ham, Round, Bearskin, Gunflint, Poplar, and Seagull Lakes are jumping-off points to hundreds of routes that are ideal for those who are just getting their sea legs. Appendix 5 (the McKenzie map index) provides an overview of this region.

If you want to get away from the crowds, begin your trip on big Saganaga Lake and paddle north into Quetico Provincial Park (you can arrange a motorized tow to the edge of the park). For still greater isolation and adventure, try the remote Ontario lakes which lie just outside the Boundary Waters. These provincial waterways are not subject to BWCA or Quetico park regulations—which means you can camp and build fires where you please. It's doubtful you will see another canoeist.

If you're new to the Boundary Waters, you'll want to choose a *wind-protected route that is easy to navigate*. Some great "circle" (no auto shuttle needed) trips originate off the Gunflint and Sawbill Trails and between Highway 1 and the Fernberg Road, just southeast of Ely.

Maps

You may choose from United States Geological Survey (USGS) and/or Canadian topographic maps, or BWCA/Quetico-specific McKenzie and W. A. Fisher Company maps. U.S. and Canadian government topo maps are very accurate but they don't show the location of portages, campsites, and hiking trails in the Boundary Waters and Quetico. For this reason, McKenzie and W. A. Fisher Company maps are preferred.

McKenzie Company Maps

McKenzie maps are drawn on a scale of 2" to the mile (1:31,680), and are printed on waterproof and nearly indestructible POLYART 2 or TYVEK paper. They have crystal-clear contour lines and declination diagrams that show the angular difference between true and magnetic north. McKenzie maps are nearly identical to those used by BWCA forest rangers. The scale makes it easy to interpret fractional one-mile, half-mile, and quarter-mile distances. McKenzie maps are my personal choice whenever I canoe the Boundary Waters. Call McKenzie at (800) 749–2113 for a free index to maps of the BWCA and Quetico.

W. A. Fisher Company Maps

W. A. Fisher Company maps are printed on waterproof, polypropylene-based paper. Scales range from ⅓ inch = 1 mile to 3½ inches = 1 mile. Most canoeists choose the contoured "F" series maps, which are drawn on a scale of 1½ inches to the mile. Fisher Company offers a nice planning book that contains fifteen non-contoured, non-waterproof maps of the BWCA/Quetico.

Write for a free index to maps covering the region you plan to travel. You'll need the Minnesota index to order USGS topographic maps. Index #1 is required for Ontario provincial maps. McKenzie and W. A. Fisher indexes cover the entire BWCA/Quetico. Procurement information for all maps is in Appendix 2.

If You Plan To Use a GPS

GPS or "Global Positioning System" units are catching on like mad! Twenty-four orbiting satellites continually transmit positioning information—latitude, longitude, elevation, and precise time (via an atomic clock)—that may be accessed by a small electronic receiver, called a "GPS." Or, you can enter a set of coordinates of a place you want to go and the GPS receiver will provide a "go to" compass bearing and distance, which will be updated by satellite information as you paddle. Press a button and you get an estimated time of arrival (ETA).

Even without a map, a GPS is extremely useful. Enter your starting position and save it as a "waypoint." Establish other waypoints as you proceed, then, like Hansel and Gretel, follow your electronic "bread crumbs" home. Some GPS units include a built-in map, which isn't detailed enough for canoe travel. However, nearly all GPS units have a "track-back" feature, which will reverse your route and guide you—leg by leg—back to your starting point.

The downside is that handheld GPS units are battery powered, so satellite tracking time is limited to the life of the small batteries. For this reason, it's impractical to leave a GPS on for continuous positioning. The most useful GPS feature is its ability to verify your location on a map, which is possible *only* if your map has a coordinate system to which the GPS can relate! U.S. and Canadian topographic maps are marked with degrees of latitude and longitude that a GPS can identify. Canadian topographic maps and many U.S. maps also use the Universal Transverse Mercator (UTM) system, which is simpler because it's decimal oriented. Neither McKenzie nor Fisher Company maps have useful GPS coordinates, so you'll need a U.S. or Canadian topographic map to plot your position. Some computer software companies offer GPS-coordinate-equipped maps of the Boundary Waters on CD ROM. Check them out if you use a GPS.

When the military discovered that GPS receivers were more accurate than they expected, they became concerned that an enemy might use a GPS to target missiles. They consequently introduced a random error of 15 to 100 meters into the civilian GPS signal. This means that locating an obscure campsite in a hidden bay still requires accurate map and compass work. Chapter 3 explains the navigational techniques you need to know.

Don't Turn Your Vacation into a Marathon!

Unless you're a marathon paddler and have a sleek, fast canoe, you'll probably cruise along at around 3 miles an hour. Subtract 1 mile per hour for gawking time, photo time, and talking time, and you reduce your average to *2 miles per hour*. To determine the actual mileage you can cover in a day, you'll have to include time lost on the portages.

Begin by adding up the *total* length, in *rods*, of the portages you will make each day. One rod equals 16.5 feet, or about the length of a typical canoe. There are 320 rods to the mile. Most physically fit canoeists can portage a canoe 160 rods or a half mile in ten to fifteen minutes, with one short rest stop. A one-mile portage (320 rods) can usually be completed in twenty to twenty-five minutes, with two or three rest stops, but the time will vary with conditions and your fitness. It won't take you long to discover that "time under the yoke" is more important than portage length. An easy 320-rod portage may be completed in less time than a tough 240-rod portage!

Table 2-1: Approximate Time in Minutes To Portage Your Gear

Map Distance	Actual Distance You'll Portage*	Easy Trail	Moderately Difficult, Uphill Trail	Very Difficult Trail
80 rods or 0.25 miles	240 rods or 0.75 miles	15	18	22
160 rods or 0.5 miles	480 rods or 1.5 miles	30	36	44
240 rods or 0.75 miles	720 rods or 2.25 miles	45	54	66
320 rods or 1.0 miles	960 rods or 3.0 miles	60	72	88

* rods x 3

Super humans may complete portages in a single grueling carry, but mere mortals like me require *two* trips, which means walking each portage *three* times, once without gear! Long, steep trails require frequent rest stops. Swamps, hills, rain, boulders, overhanging vegetation, and a crowded or precarious landing also slow you down. Some BWCA portages have wooden canoe rests (they will be removed under the new management plan) that allow you to take a breather without setting the canoe down. Where overhead rests don't exist, you'll have to shove the bow of your canoe into a tree or set the craft on the ground. Both procedures waste energy and time. For these reasons, it's probably meaningless to suggest approximate portage times. Nonetheless, these values—which assume you'll retrace your steps three times—work well enough for planning purposes.

So much for academics. How do you know if a portage or route is hard or easy? You don't! But there are some clues. One is a comparison of the elevation of the lake you're on and the one(s) you'll portage into (**Figure 2-2**). For example, suppose you're located on Warclub Lake (elev. 1693 feet). You plan to paddle up the Chub River and take the short, 45-rod portage into Glee Lake (elev. 1729 feet). The difference in elevation is 36 feet over a horizontal distance of 743 feet (45 rods x 16.5 feet per rod). That's 3.6 feet of rise for every 74 feet you walk—pretty significant, even though the portage is only 45 canoe lengths long. Make no mistake, this is a sweaty uphill grade all the way!

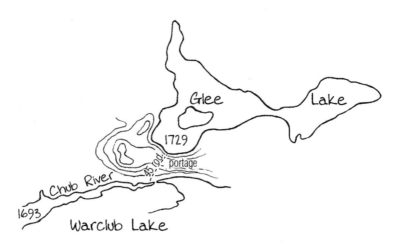

Figure 2-2. You can estimate the difficulty of a portage by comparing the elevation of two lakes on either end of the trail.

You can also check the spacing of the thin, brown contour lines on your topographic map. Contour lines indicate the elevation above sea level of land features and thus permit you to view the topography in three dimensions instead of two. These rules will help you interpret contour lines:

Rules for Interpreting Contour Lines

1. Contour lines connect points of equal elevation. Thus, closely spaced lines indicate lots of elevation change, whereas widely spaced lines show the opposite (**Figure 2-3**). You gain or lose elevation only when you travel from one contour line to another. If you walk along a contour line, you'll be "on the level."

2. The contour interval is the vertical distance in feet or meters between contour lines. Contours on all BWCA area maps are drawn at 20-foot intervals. Thus, you go 20 feet up or down whenever you walk from one contour line to another. Each fifth contour line is darkened and labeled with its actual elevation above sea level.

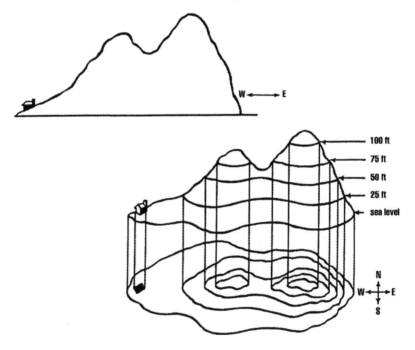

Figure 2-3. Contour lines are the key to judging the steepness of the terrain.

3. The numerical value of the contour interval (CI) is clearly stated in the margin of all U.S., Canadian, and McKenzie topographic maps, but not on W. A. Fisher Company maps, which are labeled, "…not intended for navigational use." An employee of the Fisher Company said that liability concerns required the omission of this important information.

No map is perfectly accurate. River patterns change, water levels rise and fall, trails become overgrown, shorelines erode, campsites come and go. Some USGS maps—from which most other U.S. maps are made—were last field-checked in the 1950s! No map company can keep up with all the changes imposed by nature and man. Good judgment is essential on any canoe trip!

4. Where contour lines cross or run very close together, you'll find an abrupt drop—a falls, cliff, or canyon.

5. A contour line forms a v whenever it crosses a stream or river. The closed end of the v always points upstream. Contours enable you to tell at a glance the direction of water flow (**Figure 2-4**).

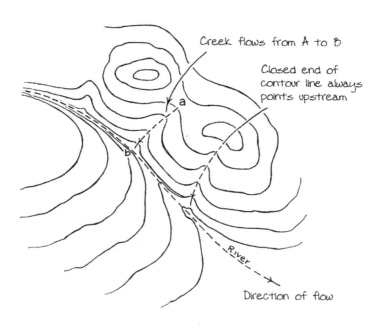

Figure 2-4. Use contour lines to determine the direction and pace of river's flow.

Planning the Route

Now that we have all the facts, let's finish planning our trip. We have decided on a travel zone (Ely, Tofte, Grand Marais...and a route that sparks our interest. The following "thought list" will help us implement the details of our scenario: seven days on the water, an interesting and diverse route, a few tough portages, five-hour paddling days, relative isolation, and one layover day.

Scenario Thought List

Have you outlined a circle route that will bring you back to your starting point, or arranged for a local outfitter to shuttle your car to the take-out? Most BWCA paddlers prefer the freedom of a circle route. You can, of course, simply paddle out the same way you came in—a less-than-adventurous experience.

Most canoe parties begin their trips on a weekend. You'll enjoy a less crowded experience if you start on a weekday.

Plan to camp within two hours' paddle of the take-out on your last day. You may be too tired to drive home if you don't!

Commit mostly to small, easy-to-navigate waters that are protected from high winds. Next year, when you have more confidence, you can try some bigger lakes. There are usually lots of portages (and sometimes more mosquitoes!) along downsized routes, so many canoeists avoid them. The result is a more remote experience for those who are occasionally willing to "sweat and swat." The scenery on sheltered routes is often punctuated with waterfalls, beaver ponds, wildlife sightings, and small, runnable rapids—experiences that are foreign to big water.

Figure on a maximum travel distance of 10 miles per day, which includes the "triple carry" length of each portage you'll make (you'll walk each portage three times, remember?). Add up the length of the portages in rods and multiply by three. Convert this figure to miles (divide rods by 320) and add it to the distance you'll paddle. Say your total is 71 miles. Your "time and distance" schedule might look something like **Table 2-2.**

Note that you've walked 18 of the 71 miles, or more than 25 percent of the way. This 75–25 ratio is fairly realistic for trips in sheltered waters. You can probably dispense with a "time and distance" schedule if you allow *at least* one-fourth of your traveling time for portaging! You can see why a lightweight canoe and outfit are so important!

You can travel with the current or against it. Your friends want to run some rapids, so you'd best go with the flow. Besides, you can often avoid some

Table 2-2 Time and Distance Schedule

Day	Time Paddling/ Portaging	Miles Paddled (at 2 mph)	Miles Portaged (length of portage x 3)	Distance
Day 1 (Tuesday)	4.5 hours	7	3	10 miles
Day 2 (Wednesday)	5 hours	8	3	11 miles
Day 3 (Thursday)	5 hours	6	6	12 miles
Day 4 (Friday)	7 hours	13	1.5	14.5 miles
Day 5 (Saturday)	None—layover day	0	0	0 miles
Day 6 (Sunday)	5 hours	8	3	11 miles
Day 7 (Monday)	4 hours	7	1.5	8.5 miles
Day 8 (Tuesday)	2 hours—out	4	0	4 miles
Total	32.5 hours	53	18	71 miles

portages by selecting a downstream route. Remember, the contour lines tell you the direction of flow; the closed end or tip of the **v** always points upstream!

Permits

Travel permits are required for canoeing the Boundary Waters. The quota permit season runs from May 1 through September 30. Self-issuing permits are required for day trips and for overnight trips between October 1 and April 30. The rules and rationale are explained in Chapter 5. For now, you need only know that the maximum party size is *nine* people and *four* canoes. There are no exceptions, even if you paddle a solo canoe or kayak.

Rules and procedures have changed in recent years, and things continue to evolve. The good news is that BWCA managers have gone high-tech and have placed everything you need to know on the Internet.

You must obtain your travel permit from the BWCAW Reservation Office, which is now part of the National Recreation Reservation Service (NRRS).

BWCAW Reservation Office
P.O. Box 462, Ballston, NY 12020
Phone: (877) 550–6777 (toll free)
Fax: (518) 884–9951
TDD: (877) TDD-NRRS (toll free)

Or, if you have a computer on line, punch up the NRRS web site, www.bwcaw.org, and follow the instructions on the screen. The Superior National Forest web site (www.fs.fed.us/r9/superior) is for Boundary Waters information only. All permits go must through the BWCAW Reservation Office in Ballston, New York.

It currently costs $9.00 to reserve a permit. There is also a "per person per trip" charge of $10.00 per adult, $5.00 per youth, and $5.00 for Golden Age and Golden Access cardholders. A seasonal fee card is available for $40 for an adult or $20 for youths and Golden Age and Golden Access cardholders.

Reserved Overnight Permits

You may reserve your overnight camping permit weeks or months before your trip. You will receive computerized verification of your travel dates, entry point, and route. You must pick up your reserved permit in person (bring the letter of confirmation) at the location you specify when you make your reservation. A new rule requires that you provide personal identification, such as a driver's license. There are dozens of permit pickup points and the BWCA brochure lists them all. Generally, permits can be picked up only during business hours, so plan accordingly!

Reserved Day-Use Motor Permits

This permit allows you to use a motor on your canoe for *one* day during the week of your canoe trip. Weeks run Saturday to Friday. Be sure you have the confirmation letter with you when you pick up your permit.

Walk-In Overnight and Day-Use Motor Permits

Stop at any Forest Service district office or any cooperating outfitter within 24 hours of your trip. If a permit is available, one will be issued to you.

You Must License Your Canoe in Minnesota

Your canoe must be licensed with the Minnesota Department of Natural Resources unless it has already been licensed in another state, in which case there must be an official decal affixed to the hull. Canoe licenses are available by mail from the Minnesota Department of Natural Resources, License Bureau, 500

Lafayette Square, St. Paul, Minnesota 55146, and from some local outfitters. Call the DNR's toll-free number, (800) 285–2000, for a list of participating outfitters. The cost is $14.00 for three years.

If you are renting a canoe in Minnesota, it has already been licensed.

Entry into Canada's Quetico Provincial Park

There are no designated campsites, fireplaces, or maintained toilets in the interior of Quetico Provincial Park. The maximum group size is nine people and there is no restriction on the number of canoes per party. The interior of Quetico is much wilder than the most remote parts of the BWCA.

Park reservations are accepted by mail beginning January 18 and by phone starting February 1. Inquiries about entry points, canoeing and camping regulations, permits, fees, licenses, and customs procedures should be addressed to:

> Quetico Provincial Park
> Ministry of Natural Resources
> 108 Saturn Avenue
> Atikokan, Ontario
> Canada P0T 1C0
> Phone (U.S. residents): (807) 597–2735
> Phone (Canadian residents): (807) 597–2737

Quetico Camping Permits

You can reserve a canoe camping permit up to eleven months in advance of your trip by calling (888) ONT-PARK. This new toll-free number became effective in 1999 and is operational twenty-four hours a day, every day. Yes, you will speak to a real person!

The Ontario Parks web site, www.ontarioparks.com, provides tips, trail maps, and virtual tours of Ontario Parks. Electronic permit reservations may be available through this Internet site by the time you read this.

American residents who have specific questions about canoeing or hiking in Quetico Provincial Park should call the Quetico Park District Manager at (807) 597–2735. Canadians should call (807) 597–2737.

To hear a recorded message about ice-out, campfire restrictions, forest fire activity, water levels, and other current park information, call (807) 597–4602. Or check the Quetico web site: www.mnr.gov.on.ca/MNR/parks.

Park fees vary according to age (youth, adult, or senior citizen), season, and facilities used. There's a daily parking charge for vehicles. You'll need to buy an Ontario angling license if you plan to fish. And you *must* check through

Canadian customs before you enter the park. Customs stations are located on Saganaga Lake (Cache Bay), Basswood Lake (Prairie Portage), and Sand Point Lake. Everything is clearly explained in the free Quetico Wilderness Guide, which available from the MNR office at the address above.

Your planning is now complete. All that remains is to assemble your food and gear and to learn how to use your newly acquired maps to find your way around the sprawling lakes you'll soon encounter.

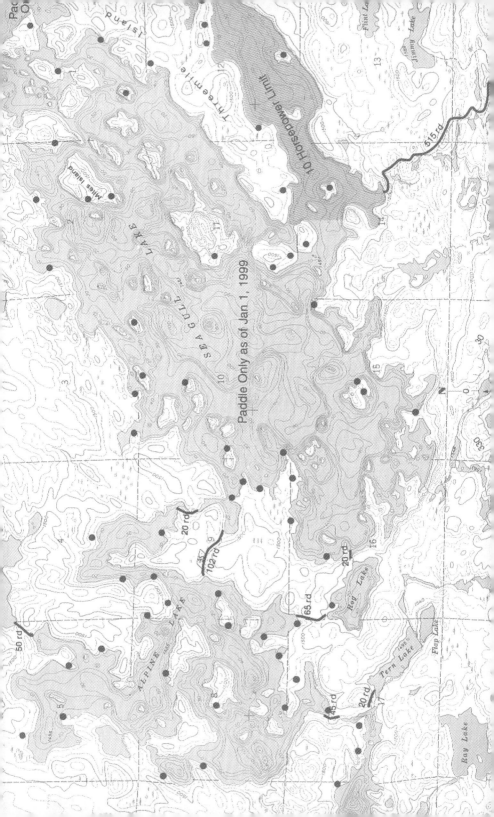

A Maze of Finger Lakes, Portage Trails, and Confusing Bays!

Newcomers to the Boundary Waters secretly admit a deep fear of being unable to find designated campsites and portages. Anxiety grows to ulcer proportions when bad weather carves hours out of a tight time schedule. To eliminate confusion, some novices simply glue their route to a shoreline or camp within sight of their starting point or a portage. Others pack away their map and compass and paddle off confidently in the general direction of their goal without giving the matter a second thought.

During the peak of the canoeing season, you can probably get around fine with either of these approaches if you have a friendly smile and a willingness to ask directions of other paddlers you meet. But you won't grow with the sport or develop much confidence in your route-finding ability. More importantly, you may lock yourself out of traveling the most remote portions of the Boundary Waters, where good map and compass reading are essential.

Ask an experienced canoeist for directions and you will almost always be politely and cheerfully accommodated. You will, however, be viewed as an incompetent bozo who doesn't know the ropes and isn't willing to take the time to learn!

Admittedly, the BWCA is not an easy place to find your way around. The maze of islands, bays, and channels, combined with portage trails that are sometimes incorrectly plotted on maps, often confuses experts who have superior map and compass skills. Indeed, my own experience on the sprawling waterways of northern Canada suggests that if you can correctly navigate complex Boundary Waters lakes like Seagull and Saganaga, you can probably find your way around any liquid habitat in the world. The BWCA may be small potatoes compared to the giant lakes of northern Canada, but the rules for navigating them are the same. A good map, a reliable *orienteering* compass, and an understanding of basic route-finding principles will eliminate confusion.

Maps

Get the best maps available. I prefer the large-scale McKenzie maps suggested in Chapter 2. Losing a map can be serious, so always carry one or two spares. The best place to store your map is in a sturdy nylon map case, under a "shock-corded" canoe thwart, as suggested in Chapter 6. Excellent map cases are available from Cooke Custom Sewing, Grade VI, and Granite Gear. Addresses are in Appendix 2.

Orienteering Compass

If you've never used an orienteering compass, you have a pleasant surprise coming. You don't have to write down numbers, memorize dial readings, or draw north-south reference lines on your map. The features you need for computing map bearings and following them on the ground are built right into the instrument!

Silva, Suunto, and Brunton all make excellent orienteering compasses. Prices range from about ten dollars to more than forty for professional models, which feature declination adjustments, night sights, and interchangeable map scales. But, you don't need any of these sophisticated features for navigating the Boundary Waters! The least expensive orienteering compasses are adequate for serious route-finding.

Inexpensive orienteering compasses are usually lighter and more compact than large-frame professional models—an advantage when you have to carry them all day in your pants pocket. My favorite Boundary Waters compass is the tiny (and inexpensive) Nexus 27LU, which is scarcely larger than a book of paper matches.

Carry a spare compass "just in case." A small wrist compass attached with a strap or Velcro to a canoe thwart provides instant bearings while you paddle. A thwart-mounted "running" compass simplifies direction finding and may even promote your safe passage. For example, say you're following a compass heading across a windy lake. You paddle around an island and momentarily lose track of your direction. If you put down your paddle and reach for your orienteering compass to check the course, you may broadside the waves and swamp. Your thwart-mounted "running" compass will show the way quickly—and safely.

No Need to Worry about Magnetic Declination!

A compass needle points to *magnetic* north, not *true* north. The angular difference between the two norths is called "declination." In some areas of the

United States—notably the far east and west, declination can be as much as twenty-one degrees! Fortunately, declination in the BWCA and adjacent Quetico Provincial Park is so small (it ranges from about three degrees at the eastern edge of the BWCA to a bit more than four degrees at the western boundary) that you can ignore it.

For example: One degree of compass error equals 92 feet per mile of ground error. Say you shoot a compass bearing from your location to a point one-half mile away. This is a fairly long compass shot, given the small size of most Boundary Waters lakes. Figure in an area maximum declination of four degrees east, and you would be off course a maximum of 184 feet (92 feet per mile x 4 degrees x 0.5 mile) or about half the length of a football field—hardly enough to cause concern.

So rest easy, there is no need to correct compass readings for declination in the BWCA!

Using Map and Compass Together

In order to locate portages and campsites, you must know, within reason, where you are at all times. This means you must proceed along an established direction, or "bearing" as it is called.

Assume you are camped at point A on Whiskey Jack Lake (**Figure 3-1**). Your destination is portage X in the southwest corner of Trout Bay. Getting to X should be easy: Just head southwest through the channel at B, then curve around Moose Island until you come to the lake expanse. Now turn south, cross to the opposite shore, and follow your nose to the portage. Easy as pie!

Don't you believe it! Look at the map scale. It's about three-eighths of a mile to the channel at B, and nearly a full mile from Moose Island to the mainland at G. Even on a clear day, it's hard to discern the nature of islands, channels, and bays that are hundreds of yards away. Add morning fog, wind, and waves, plus the sight and sounds of unfamiliar surroundings, and you could easily become confused. Better to resort to precise compass bearings and follow a systematic plan. The important thing is to know your location at all times—easy enough if you compute compass bearings to intermediate checkpoints (B, C, D, E, etc.) along the way and verify your position when you arrive at each point. Here's the procedure:

First arbitrarily pick a checkpoint on the map. It should be some place that's reasonably close (preferably within one-half mile of your location) and easily identifiable—a small island, the tip of a peninsula, a prominent bay, or such. You

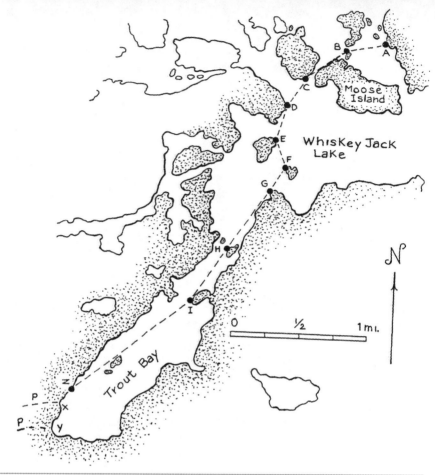

Figure 3-1. Whiskey Jack Lake and Trout Bay

probably won't be able to see your checkpoint from your distant location.

Let's say that the island at B (the dot marks the point) is your first checkpoint. Don't touch your compass until you first estimate (within ninety degrees) the bearing from A to B. You'll be heading roughly west, so your computed compass bearing should be around 270 degrees.

Now use your orienteering compass to determine the actual compass bearing from A to B. **Figure 3-2** shows the procedure:

> **1.** Place either the left or right edge of the compass base plate over point A. Place the forward edge of the same side of the base plate on point B. Your compass is now pointing in the direction you want to go—from A to B not from B to A!

2. While holding the base plate tightly in position, turn the compass housing until north on the dial points to north (the top) on the map. Your direction of travel—256 degrees—is now locked on the dial and can be read at the index inscribed on the compass base. Don't use the magnetic needle!

Stop. Do not continue until you have compared your computed compass bearing to your earlier estimate! The most common mistakes are quadrant errors (90–180 degrees) and full 180-degree errors. You'll avoid these embarrassing mistakes if you compare your calculated bearing to your estimate before you start paddling! The two figures should closely agree. Your calculated bearing of 256 degrees is within forty-five degrees of your 270-degree estimate, so it's unlikely you made a serious mistake.

It's easier to make a large computational error than you think! For exam-

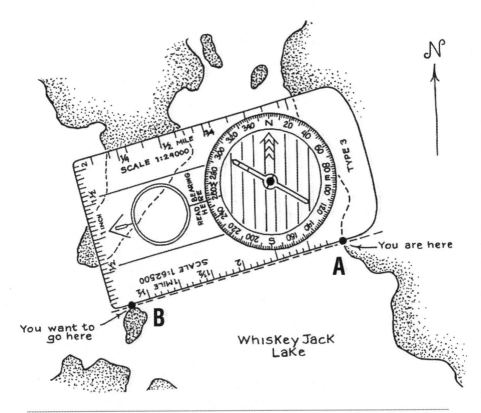

Figure 3-2. Double check your calculated bearings, your estimated bearings, and the distance before you set off.

ple, if you inadvertently place your compass wrong on the map or turn the north arrow on the housing down (south) instead of up (north), your computed bearing may be off by 180 degrees!

3. Now . . . while holding the compass in front of you with the direction-of-travel arrow inscribed on the base plate pointing *away* from your body, rotate your body *with the compass* until the magnetic needle points to north on the dial. Look straight ahead. You are now facing 256 degrees—toward B.

4. All that's necessary now is to locate a notch or incongruity on the horizon that you can identify as being on this course of travel. Put your compass away and start paddling! Remember that wind may blow your canoe off course, so don't follow a bearing set on your thwart-mounted compass. Instead, select a point on the horizon that is in line with the bearing you computed with your orienteering compass.

Test Your Map and Compass Skills

Test time! Use your orienteering compass and Figure 3-1 to test your knowledge of "point to point" navigation. Remember to estimate the bearing to each point before you compute it! Consider your answers correct if they are within three degrees of those given in Table 3.1 at the end of this chapter.

If you can successfully navigate Whiskey Jack Lake (Figure 3-1), you'll be "on course" on your next canoe trip. That's a promise!

Aiming Off

Maps are made from aerial photos, and the plane-mounted camera can only record what it sees. Man-made features like portages are often obscured by trees, so the cartographer has to guess at precise locations. As water levels fluctuate, shorelines change shape. The result is that what you see on the map may not accurately represent what is on the ground. To locate a misplotted feature, you'll need to "aim off."

For example: You are located at point I on Whiskey Jack Lake (Figure 3-1), and you want to go to portage X. If this portage is incorrectly plotted on the map, or you make a small compass error, you could miss your objective. Err much to the south and you could even mistake portage Y for X!

The solution is to "aim off"—that is, make a purposeful error to the right or left of X. In the example, an arbitrary point (Z) was selected. Determine the bear-

Table 3.1: Answers to the Test

From	Your Guestimate	Actual Compass Bearing
A to B	SW (180°–270°)	256°
B to C	SW (180°–270°)	237°
C to D	SW (180°–270°)	216°
D to E	S (about 180°)	196°
E to F	SE (90°–180°)	162°
F to G	SW (180°–270°)	211°
G to H	SW (180°–270°)	217°
H to I	SW (180°–270°)	217°
I to Z, just north of portage X[a]	SW (180°–270°)	234°

[a]Note that this bearing was computed to an arbitrary point (Z) just north of portage X. This *aiming off* procedure prevents undershooting or overshooting of your objective.

ing from I to Z and start paddling! You will intersect the shoreline somewhere *north* of X. Follow the shore south to the first portage you come to. That's X. What could be simpler?

"Aim off" whenever you use your compass and you won't spend hours searching for portages!

Tips for Navigating Small Streams and Moose Trails

Sometimes you can bypass portages by following a connecting stream or moose trail to the next lake. Here are some hints for navigating these meandering waterways:

1. Where a stream forks, take the route with the strongest flow, even if it looks more restrictive than a broader channel. If there's no discernible current, note which way the grass bends in the channel and follow.

2. Check your compass frequently; don't rely on your map!

3. If you come to a dead end and see a trail, scout it before you carry your canoe across. Your "portage" may turn out to be an animal path that leads to a connecting tributary or dead-end pond.

Favorite Routes – Where Solitude Still Remains

I live on the Minnesota border where snow stays on the ground from November to May. When melt water finally comes to Viking land, there's cause for celebrating. Canoes and camping gear that have lain dormant all winter are suddenly the focus of attention, as everyone prepares for the elusive summer. May 15, start of the fishing opener, officially marks the end of the ice age in Minnesota, and the first big influx of visitors to the BWCA. Fortunately, most serious anglers limit their casts to large, accessible lakes like Rainy, Vermillion, Basswood, Seagull, and Saganaga, where motors are permitted and portages are non-existent. That leaves lots of space for winter-crazed paddlers like me who want to get away from the crowds.

Long, rough portages once separated serious backwoods travelers from wilderness weenies. Today, lightweight gear has evened the score—a one-mile portage is easy if you have a fifty-pound canoe and Spartan kit. Just about everyone who canoes the Boundary Waters these days has discovered the light-weight advantage. Those who haven't are quickly set straight by area outfitters who offer the latest in ultralight gear. "Getting away from it all" now means probing deeper into the wilderness than ever before, or cleverly skirting the beaten path (more on this later).

You *can* find solitude in the Boundary Waters if you portage into a dead-end lake, pond-hop between beaver streams, or select a route that includes hard-to-portage rapids. Whitewater terrifies unskilled paddlers, especially those who have sleek, fragile, cruising canoes that turn only reluctantly. Deviate from the programmed portage path (even momentarily!) and you'll discover that there's a wild and woolly side to the BWCA.

Here are a few of my favorite haunts and some adventurous ways to get away from the crowd:

Ham Lake to Long Island Lake and Points East (Figure 4-1)

Time: three to seven days
Maps: McKenzie #7 and #4, or Fisher #114 or F-13 and F-6

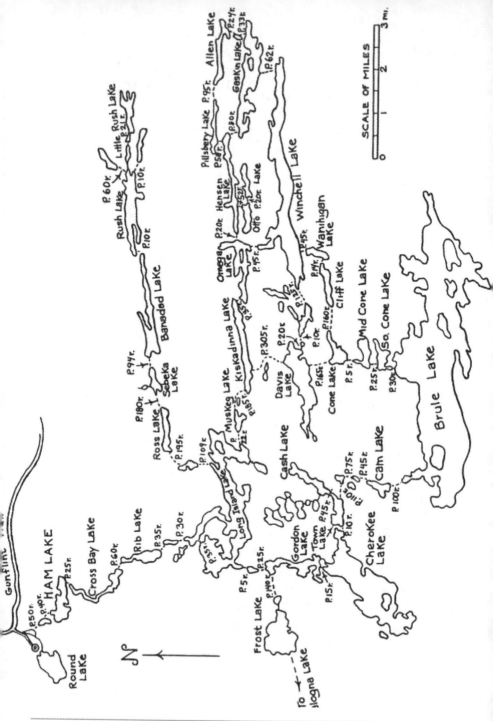

Figure 4-1. The Ham Lake to Long Island Lake Route.

Here's a diverse route for those who prefer small, easily navigable (you can't get lost!), wind-protected lakes that have nice campsites, good fishing, and lots of wildlife.

Enter at Ham Lake off the Gunflint Trail near Grand Marais. It's an easy day's paddle to Long Island Lake, via Cross Bay, Rib, George, and Karl Lakes. There's a long sand beach (rare, in this region of uninterrupted granite!) at the end of the 35-rod portage from Karl Lake to Long Island Lake.

If you want a more remote experience, exit Long Island Lake to the east and paddle into Ross, Banadad, and Rush Lakes. Or, drop down into Muskeg, Omega, Hensen, and Pillsberry. Loop back to Long Island Lake through Winchell and Davis, or cut south to big Brule Lake, and return by way of Cam, Town, and Cherokee Lakes. Surrounded by high granite cliffs, tiny Cam Lake looks, from the seat of a canoe, like a crater hole. It is one of the most beautiful and unusual spots in the area. Several tight, annoying portages keep most people away.

The skinny streams that feed Long Island Lake are prime habitat for beaver, moose, otter, and muskrat. The region feels comfortably intimate—a perfect place for adventurous beginners who are just spreading their wings.

Frost River (figure 4-2)

Time: five to seven days
Maps: McKenzie #7 and #8, or Fisher #113 and #114 or F-12, F-13, F-19

The Frost River has a smattering of everything—large and small lakes; beautiful falls; winding beaver streams and high beaver dams; tough, poorly maintained portages; canoeable rapids; and adventurous options. It is by far my favorite route in the Boundary Waters.

The Frost River is rugged and isolated. You'll enjoy the trip more if you have lightweight gear, a compact kit, and an unhurried attitude. You'll paddle downhill all the way and enjoy a number of easy rapids. Campsites are limited on the Frost River portion of the route, so you'd best plan your stays accordingly. The trip *must* be done in early June or late September when water levels are reasonably high.

Expect to see lots of wildlife. When my wife, Susie, and I paddled the Frost in our solo canoes in June 1993, we saw five otters, one beaver, several muskrats, a white-tailed deer (!) and two huge bull moose. We were too rushed to fish, though on past trips (I've paddled the Frost at least a dozen times) we've nabbed some nice smallmouth bass and northern pike.

Park your car at the Round Lake public landing (**Figure 4-1**), and begin your

Figure 4-2. The Frost River Route.

trip at Ham Lake, a five-minute walk to the east. Paddle south to Long Island Lake, then take the 140-rod portage into Frost Lake. This portage is long and mean so I usually camp at Long Island or Gordon Lake and save the sweaty carry for the next morning. There are only two campsites between Frost Lake and the mouth of the river at Afton Lake. Bologna Lake, which is accessed by a short, ten-rod portage has one campsite, and it's a knockout!

The Frost River valley is well protected from wind and the sounds of other paddlers. There are several small waterfalls, rapids, and beaver dams to portage. You'll thread your way through miles of head-high vegetation, twisting and turning with the restricted flow. Fortunately, beavers and moose maintain a tight but navigable channel.

In good weather, it's twelve to fourteen hours from Frost Lake to Little Saganaga Lake, and you'll spoil the fun if you do it all in a single day. The winding Frost River is so remote and inspiring that two days are hardly enough for those who contemplate and explore the waterway. Only one portage intersects the river—a grueling 300-rodder out of Hub Lake. Fellow voyageurs are either behind you or ahead and gone.

At Whipped Lake, you may choose to head north to Mora, Gillis, Chub River, and Brant, ending your trip at Round Lake. Or proceed north to Gabimichigami, Ogishkemuncie, Jasper, Alpine, and Seagull.

The first option is much more remote and adventurous, especially if you bypass the 100-rod portage to Mora and take the obscure Time Lake cutoff. The rapids and swifts between Whipped and Mora Lakes can all be run, lined, or portaged. Be sure you have ropes attached to the bow and stern of your canoe!

Little Saganaga Lake is one of the most beautiful in the Boundary Waters. It is well worth seeing, even though it is very heavily traveled. You're on big water now, as you loop north toward famed Seagull Lake. The country is gorgeous, portages are easy, and there are plenty of other canoeists around. "Remote" defines country you've left behind! Any of the area's outfitters will shuttle your car from Ham Lake to Seagull for a small charge.

Granite River through Guide's Portage (Figure 4-3)

Time: three to five days
Access: via Gunflint Trail, north of Grand Marais

The Granite River is one of the most beautiful and satisfying routes in the Boundary Waters. Portages are short and well maintained, the high granite bluffs discourage wind, and the high relief topography is truly spectacular. It's a downstream run all the way to Saganaga Lake, which for all practical purposes is the only big water on the route. The route is easy to navigate.

The downside is that *lots* of very inexperienced people canoe the Granite River. In fact, just about every tripping camp in the region sends its teen groups down the Granite. Use—and abuse—is heavy. Most of the "good wood" on campsites has been picked over and, more often than not, campsites are at or nearly at full capacity. Nonetheless, the Granite River is so rewarding that you'll want to paddle it more than once.

Begin your trip at the public landing on Gunflint Lake. Arrange with Gunflint Lodge to shuttle your car to Trail's End landing on Saganaga Lake. Paddle north to Pine Portage but *don't* carry into Clove Lake. Instead, descend

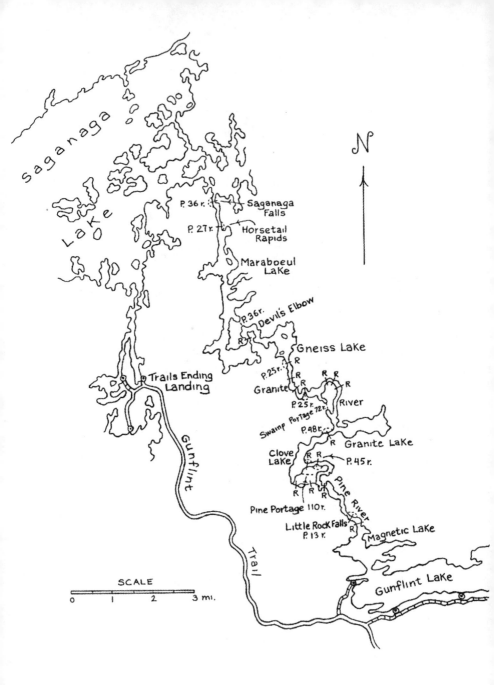

Figure 4-3. The Granite River route.

through a small swift and follow the main body of the river into a quiet pool that dead-ends about 100 yards above Clove Lake. An unkempt portage begins on river left (the American side) at the head of a rapid. The rapid ends at a substantial falls, below which is one of the most beautiful spots—and best swimming holes—I've seen. Near the left shore, a natural bathtub is carved into the hard, smooth granite. You can't camp at the falls, but you can picnic, swim, and nap.

Follow the portage to the quiet pool below the falls. Then, paddle across the pool to the Canadian side and hoist your outfit about ten feet up the rock embankment to the overgrown trail above. A five-minute walk down "Guide's Portage" brings you to Clove Lake. Most people take the 100-rod portage directly to Clove Lake and miss the falls, which I think is the prettiest spot on the Granite River. "Guides Portage" was named for the commercial guides who, decades ago, brought clients here to fish below the falls. The area is fragile, so please pass through quietly, and clean and carry out any mess you find. In return, you'll experience one of the premier attractions of the BWCA.

At the end of Clove Lake is an innocuous-looking rapid. A fast right turn is needed to get around the midstream boulder that sits in the heart of the flowing water. *Study* this rapid before you attempt it. Better yet, take the good portage on river left!

As you proceed downriver, you'll come to several small rapids that are bypassed by easy portages. Many of the rapids can be run if you have whitewater experience.

Follow the Granite River to Saganaga Lake, then swing west and south and paddle to your take-out point at Trail's End landing.

Earlier in this chapter, I suggested that the Boundary Waters has a wild and woolly side that comes to light whenever you leave the beaten path. Many rapids, swifts, and beaver streams that are routinely portaged by unadventurous canoeists can, after careful inspection, be safely canoed, lined, or waded—an example is the "Time Lake cutoff" suggested earlier. *Do not run any rapid until you have walked its length, checked every turn and rock, and discussed "possible outcomes" with your partner*!

Follow a beaver stream to a dead-end lake, set a compass course, and hike overland to a landlocked pond, climb some high hills, and, as John Muir proclaimed, "Get their good tidings." Slow your pace; shorten your trip plans; investigate your options; probe shorelines, quiet bays, and the thin lines on your map; and you'll discover challenge and solitude wherever you paddle.

Federal Regulations and Rationale

Every part of the earth is sacred to my people. Every shining pine needle, every sandy shore, every mist in the dark woods, every clearing and humming insect is holy in the memory and experience of my people.

— Chief Sealth (Seattle), *from a speech delivered to representatives of the U.S. government in 1855.*

Autumn mist on an isolated lake deep in the BWCA. One last paddle trip before the icy throes of winter—a final opportunity to camp and fish and to enjoy the good times that go with warm friendships and fire-brewed coffee served steaming hot on a chilly morning.

Round the bend is the campsite that you discovered more than a decade ago. Hauntingly beautiful, it is your "special" place. You pull your canoe up on shore and follow the well-worn trail to the clearing above. The view from on top is spectacular, just as you remembered it.

Then you see them—rusty cans, aluminum foil, and candy wrappers. Torn plastic sheeting, secured to knotted nylon cord, flutters from a white birch tree whose bark has been stripped to start campfires. At the center of the stage is the steel fire grate, which is choked with green cedar branches and pine needles. Nearby, deeply eroded ruts tell you that those who last camped here "ditched" their tents to drain storm water.

Suddenly, this place is no longer special. It is a trash heap, an insult to man and God. A gnawing pain grows upward from the pit of your stomach and surfaces as rage. The spell is broken!

Fortunately, trashed campsites like these are uncommon in the Boundary Waters. Strictly enforced environmental regulations and a growing educational effort by federal authorities have eliminated most abuse. Many canoeists share an almost religious view of the Boundary Waters. They willingly clean up after themselves and others, taking personal pride as their only reward. The "bottle and can" ban has all but eliminated this once-prominent eyesore, but many of the old problems—candy wrappers, aluminum foil, stripped birch bark, vegetation-choked fire grates, and cut green trees—remain.

The "rules of travel" accompany every permit, and visitors are encouraged—newcomers are *required*—to see and reflect on a variety of educational videos, pamphlets, and photos describing low-impact camping techniques. Nonetheless, the exposure is too fast and badly timed. Wilderness education should take place in a more relaxed setting, days or weeks in advance of the outdoor experience. This is especially true where children are concerned.

The key to mastery is practice, practice, and more practice, *before* paddles touch water. To this end, I offer a unique "Wilderness Meal" cookout (see Appendix 4) that I developed for use in my eighth-grade environmental science classes. Kids (and adults!) love this non-intimidating "hands on" activity, which gets at the heart of wilderness ethics. My publisher graciously permits you to copy Appendix 4 for educational purposes, in any numbers you wish.

In order to provide a quality outdoor experience for everyone, *everyone* must understand the rationale behind each rule. They must also be armed with alternatives to environmentally unsound practices. For example: How do you keep storm water out of your tent if you can't dig a trench around it? Or make a cheery fire without using birch bark and cedar foliage? If campers know how to tie quick-release (slippery) knots that come out with a single pull, they probably won't leave knotted cord hanging from trees! Suppose that, due to circumstances beyond your control, you must camp overnight at an unapproved site. It happens! Once a tornado-like gale with winds to 65 miles per hour pinned my teenage crew on a lonely shoreline for eighteen hours. Given this scenario, how do you cook, sleep, answer the call of nature, and get out of the weather without mucking up the environment? Every Boundary Waters canoeist should know the answers to these questions and be skilled in applying environmentally sound solutions!

The rules for canoeing the Boundary Waters are clearly spelled out in the "Visitor's Guide," which is available free from the Superior National Forest office in Duluth. Here's an overview of the most important concerns.

Quotas

About 200 groups enter the Boundary Waters each day during the canoeing season, so there are strict admission quotas to ensure a quality experience for all. Fortunately, the bickering among interest groups that prevailed a few years ago has quieted, and management polices now appear to be written in soft stone—at least, for a while.

The maximum party size is nine, which is identical to that in Quetico Provincial Park. And the number of canoes that can travel together is four. The party-size regulation applies everywhere in the BWCA—on campsites, portages, and lakes. Associated groups may use the same route, but they cannot canoe together. This law is rigidly enforced!

Some Obscure Regulations

1. All members of a party must camp on the same site.

2. Sailboats and sailboards are prohibited.

3. Competitive events (like canoe and dog sled races) are prohibited.

4. Dogs are required to be under voice or leash control.

5. A Special Use Permit (Outfitter-Guide License) is required for anyone who guides private individuals, school, church, and camp groups. Of course, there's a "processing fee." It's geared to the number of clients and the number of days out. Back in the mid-1970s, our school district was required to obtain outfitter-guide licenses for staff personnel who led trips into the Boundary Waters. There was a lot of red tape and expense involved, and no check on leadership competency. Anyone who filled out the papers and paid the money got a license. The United States Forest Service (USFS) in Duluth can provide the essential forms.

No Cans or Bottles Are Allowed in the BWCA!

Foods and medicines are the only exception to this rule. Nonburnable disposable food and beverage containers are not allowed. Rigging a #10 tin can with a coat-hanger bail and using it as a cooking pot is not legal! This same rule applies in Quetico Provincial park but not on adjacent crown (public) lands.

Camouflage Your Camp

The USFS encourages you to select equipment whose colors "blend in" with the surroundings. The rationale is that a green tent or canoe is less obtrusive than a red one. However, brightly colored gear can provide an important safety advantage if you venture off the beaten path. For example, I once set my dark brown solo canoe among some willows along an obscure beaver stream in Ontario and sauntered off to scout a portage. When I returned, the canoe was "gone," or so I thought. I searched for an hour before I found it—right where I left it!

Here's another example. Four men with green canoes and earth-tone colored tents began a canoe trip on Saganaga Lake in the Boundary Waters. They paddled north through Quetico Provincial Park and arranged a float plane pickup on an Ontario lake just outside the Park. The men were at the appointed spot at the appointed time but the bush pilot never saw them, even after circling their camp-site three times. Believing that the crew was behind schedule, the pilot returned to base and searched the area again the following day. This time, the canoeists lit a smoky fire that brought the airplane down. The men paid $380 for the extra flight!

Subtle colors make sense for traditional Boundary Waters trips, but not for remote routes that may put you in harm's way. As the examples reveal, it is not always best to "blend in" with nature.

Camp Only at U.S. Forest Service Designated Sites

Shown as "red dots" on McKenzie and Fisher Company maps, designated campsites have box latrines, fire grates, and cleared tent spots. Stay away from campsites that are closed (a sign is erected)! The reason for closure may be overuse or dangerous water pollution—human waste from the box latrine may have seeped into the lake and contaminated the water. *Never swim or take drinking water from areas near closed campsites!* You'll find more particulars about water pollution and purification in Chapter 12.

When Nature Calls and There Is No Forest Service Box Latrine

When nature calls and there is no box latrine, do this: Go at least 150 feet from water, well away from campsites and portage trails. Dig a shallow (2 to 6 inches) hole with the heel of your boot. When you have finished, burn the toilet paper and *thoroughly douse* the flames with water from your poly bottle. Be care-ful: Well-meaning campers have started forest fires by burning toilet paper. Do *not* burn toilet paper if you don't have a water bottle! Cover human waste and *dead out* fire remains with 2 to 6 inches of soil. That's all there is to it!

The rationale for this procedure is that human waste and *burned* toilet paper

---

degrade quickly if microbes are present. The top 6 inches of soil contain the greatest number of decay organisms. Forest Service box latrines are environmentally unsound because they concentrate fecal matter in deep, rocky soil where there is little bacterial action. Nonetheless, box latrines are the preferred method of waste disposal because few campers willingly embrace the "heel-scrape/burn toilet paper" procedure suggested above.

Campfires Are Allowed Only Within the Steel Fire Grates at Developed Campsites

This thoroughly sensible rule is seldom violated in the BWCA. However, a secure place to contain fire is one thing; the *ability* to make it, especially in rain, is another. When repeated attempts to make fire fail, frustrated campers often strip birch bark and cedar boughs from living trees. Often, they chop or saw fully grown, live trees. My own experience suggests that *saws* have replaced axes as the favored tool of destruction. On a recent BWCA solo canoe trip, I counted fourteen sawn green trees around my camp on Bat Lake in the Gunflint Trail area.

In severe weather, a professional outdoors person, armed with matches and a Swiss army knife, may need thirty minutes or more to establish a reliable campfire. Given the same situation and tools, a novice camper may be lucky to get smoke.

In Chapter 10 you'll discover how a hand axe—the carrying of which is heavily discouraged by Boundary Waters authorities—can simplify fire-making and thereby eliminate environmental damage to living foliage.

An Unattended Fire Is Serious Cause for Concern

Just about every experienced canoeist at one time or other has passed a campsite with an actively burning campfire and no one to guard it. Because you can't control a campfire you can't see, any activity that takes everyone away from the fire site is a breach of safety and a violation of law. Leaving a fire unattended, even for short periods of time, is something that Forest Service personnel take very seriously!

Be Sure Your Fire Is Dead Out Before You Leave Camp!

Douse your campfire with plenty of water and stir the ashes to a thick slush that exudes no smoke or steam. Then, check the slurry with your hand. A popular rule is that "if the ashes are hot enough to burn your hand, they are hot enough to burn a forest!"

Sanitation and Waste Disposal

Before you retire, your food supply should be double-sealed in plastic and secured in your buckled Duluth pack. The food pack should be taken out of the immediate camp area and hidden in the woods, among rocks along the shore, or treed. There are specific instructions in Chapter 11.

The best way to dispose of uneaten food is to burn it. Build a good, hot fire so that the remains of foodstuffs won't extinguish the blaze. Burn garbage completely, and be sure to pick aluminum foil out of the flames before it melts all over everything. Partially melted foil has become the scourge of the Boundary Waters.

Soupy leftovers and fish entrails can be a problem. If you throw them in the lake, germ counts rise and dissolved oxygen levels fall. For this reason, "burial by water" is illegal in Minnesota and in most other places. The best method is to bury biodegradable wastes under 4 to 6 inches of soil, well away from camp, at least 150 feet from water. A heavy rock or log placed atop the buried remains will help discourage animals. On very isolated lakes, fish viscera may be placed on a large boulder well away from designated campsites and human habitation. Seagulls will appreciate the meal.

Dishes should be washed on land, well away from the water's edge. Ditto bathing and shampooing hair. Take dirty bathwater out of the campsite area, 150 feet from the lake, and pour it into the ground. Greasy dishwater is best poured into a shallow hole and covered with soil. Detergents should be biodegradable and sparingly used.

At the start of this chapter, I mentioned "alternatives" to environmentally unsound ways. You'll find a wealth of these procedures in the chapters that follow.

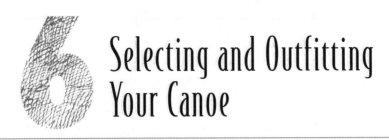

Selecting and Outfitting Your Canoe

A Boundary Waters Canoe Can Never Be Too Light!

Where the lakes end, the portages begin. They go up and down hills, over boulder fields and through swamps. Often, you must hop from rock to rock or slosh hundreds of yards through knee-high muck, balancing your canoe and swatting mosquitoes as you go. You may repeat this scenario half a dozen times on a typical day in the Boundary Waters. If you want to keep a merry disposition, you'll paddle a very light canoe!

How light is *very light*? Sixty-five pounds is reasonable, fifty-five or less is a blessing. There are tripping canoes that weigh under fifty pounds. Look into them if you want to treat your body kindly.

Surprisingly, a very small reduction in canoe weight makes a big difference on the portage trail. Alternately carry a sixty-five-pound and a sixty-pound canoe over the same portage and you'll marvel at the contrast. Try the same experiment with a loaded packsack and you'll be less impressed. Why? Because all the weight of the pack is borne by your torso, while that of the canoe is spread along the length of the hull, which affects its "swing weight" or momentum. The effect is most punishing on a tight, twisting portage where you must hop from rock to rock.

A Fast Canoe Is a Welcome Luxury

A fast canoe is a luxury, given the small lakes and frequent portages that dominate the Boundary Waters. For example, a good crew can cover a mile in a long, lean canoe in twelve to fourteen minutes. Another minute or two may be needed to propel a shorter, pushier craft—a small concern when everyone is on vacation and out for a good time.

On the other hand, it's nice to have a canoe that paddles easily, especially when you're pushing into a strong head wind. Fortunately, lightweight canoes are usually fast canoes. Why? Because lightweight construction is expensive, few manufacturers will waste it on bad design.

The variables that affect speed and ease of paddling are too complex to detail here (see my books *Canoeing & Camping* and *Canoeing Wild Rivers* for specifics). However, these rules always apply:

1. Long, skinny canoes are faster and easier to paddle than short, fat canoes. They also stay on course better in wind.

2. A keel is not necessary to keep a canoe on course. Indeed, a keel is usually the sign of an inferior canoe! Aluminum canoes which are formed in two halves and require a longitudinal brace along the bottom, are the exception. The Indians and voyageurs did not have keels on their canoes, so why should we? Straight tracking (the ability to stay on course in wind) is largely a function of long waterline length, fine ends, and a slender, rounded or vee-shaped hull form.

3. Given two canoes, identical except for their weight, the lighter canoe will accelerate faster and require less effort to maintain its speed. Only when driving forward into a head wind is the momentum of a heavier canoe an advantage.

Canoe Building Materials

Royalex and polyethylene are the preferred materials for canoes that will be used on rocky rivers. But we're paddling lake country, remember? A Boundary Waters cruiser should be light and quick—features that largely favor Kevlar, fiberglass, and wood-strip construction. However, recent advances in fabrication techniques now make Royalex a viable competitor. Check out the sleek new Royalex cruising canoes from Dagger, Old Town, Mad River, and We-no-nah, and you'll see how far this material has come.

Canoe Tips

1. If you want to round up a great Boundary Waters canoe but don't want to research hull designs, look hard at keel-less, lightweight canoes about 17½ to 18½ feet long. These craft are usually designed for serious paddlers.

2. Wood gunnels, seats, and thwarts are usually much lighter than aluminum and plastic trim. The difference may amount to as much as ten pounds on the typical 17-foot canoe! And contrary to popular belief, maintenance of wood-trimmed boats is easy. Store your craft out of direct sun and rain,

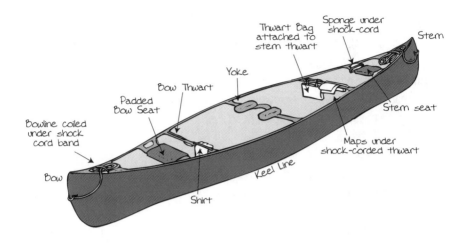

Figure 6-1. A typical set up for a Boundary Waters canoe.

occasionally rub in some Djeks Olay, linseed, or Watco oil, and the craft will
outlive you!

3. Before every trip, tighten all the bolts that secure the seats and thwarts of
your canoe. Canoes naturally flex as they are paddled, hardware works
loose, and cracks develop in the wood trim. Loose bolts are the major reason why seat frames and carrying yokes break on canoe trips!

Outfitting the Canoe

Carrying Yoke

The rugged nature of the Boundary Waters demands that a canoe be
portaged by *one* person. Two-person carries are often very painful. That's because
when one person climbs up on a rock, the other steps down. The result is a series
of shocking blows to the shoulders and spine of both partners.

It follows that your first order of business is to install a comfortable carrying
yoke in the center of your canoe. The Minnesota-style yoke, which consists of a
curved ash thwart and two thick, foam-filled shoulder pads, is by far the best. The
contoured pads of some New England–style yokes tend to gouge your shoulders
when going up and down steep hills.

Boundary Waters outfitters all equip their canoes with Minnesota-style yokes, though most aren't very good. Either the pads are too thin or they're spaced wrong for your shoulders. Occasionally, the yoke bar is mounted incorrectly, which makes for an unbalanced canoe that you'll have to carry over the portages! For this reason, you may want to make a custom-fitted yoke like the one illustrated in **Figure 6-2**. Routed slots and gunnel clamps enable you to quickly install the yoke in any canoe or remove it to provide space for bulky gear or a passenger. Indeed, a quickly removable yoke is a luxury you won't want to be without if you travel with three people in your canoe!

You can buy "Minnesota yokes" or curved ash bars from any Midwestern canoe shop, or saw a facsimile from a straight-grained *ash* board. You'll be miserable on long portages if the yoke pads aren't spaced to match the width of your shoulders. Small-framed adults should follow the dimensions suggested for teenagers. Factory yoke pads generally measure 7 inches by 3 inches. The suggested 4 by 8 pads are *much* more comfortable!

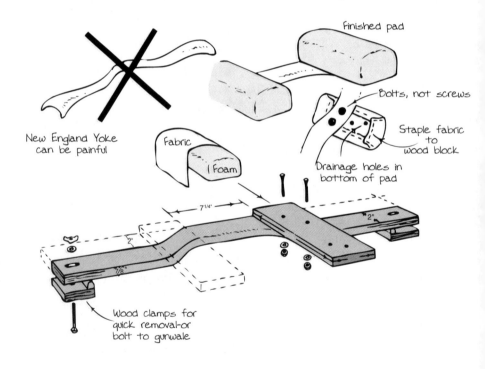

Figure 6-2. The Minnesota Yoke.

Here's a tip. If you're renting a canoe, bring along an adjustable wrench and screwdriver (slotted and Phillips) so you can unbolt the punishing metal yoke and install your own flexible wooden one!

Keep a Ready Line on Your Canoe!

Attach 10 feet of ¼-inch polypropylene rope (it floats) to each end of your canoe. Coil the ropes and secure them under bands of shock cord strung through holes on the decks, or bind them with heavy rubber bands so they won't stream out when you portage. An unexpected wind can turn your beached canoe into a kite, so be sure to tie the craft to a tree whenever you go ashore!

Tether Small Items to Canoe Thwarts

Drill holes through the thwarts and install lengths of elastic shock cord through the holes. Maps and oddities placed under the elastic bands will stay put in wind and when you portage. Duct tape shock cords to the thwarts on rental canoes.

Thwart Bags

Some paddlers place small items like bug dope, sunscreen, and munchies in a small day pack. I prefer the handiness of a zippered bag that hangs from a canoe thwart or gunnel. You can buy commercial thwart bags or make your own by sewing fasteners onto any fanny pack or light nylon briefcase.

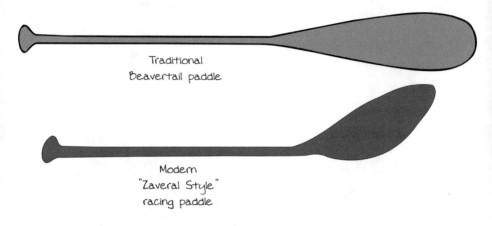

Traditional
Beavertail paddle

Modern
"Zaveral Style"
racing paddle

Figure 6-3. Two styles of canoe paddles.

Sponge

If you want to keep the bottom of your canoe looking nice, you'll bring a giant sponge! Of course, you can occasionally capsize and wash your empty canoe, but I don't recommend it. The yoke pads soak up water, stay wet for days, and leak foul-smelling liquid down your back when you portage.

Figure 6-1 shows a clever place to store your sponge.

Life Jackets

Federal and Minnesota law *requires* canoeists to have a Coast Guard–approved life vest in their canoe. You can follow the "letter of the law," or you can do what's smart—*wear your life jacket at all times while paddling*! Admittedly, everyone cheats on hot, calm days. But the rules make sense, and I urge you to stick by them. You will, if you choose a trim-fitting life vest that's cool and comfortable to wear.

Paddles

You need a lightweight paddle for making time on the big lakes, and a more durable spare for beating about rocky shallows. Serious canoeists usually choose a relatively short, twelve- to fourteen-degree "bent" paddle for fast cruising, and a somewhat longer, straight paddle for rock-dodging and maneuvering in tight areas.

Fifty-four inches is the most popular length for a bent-shaft paddle that will be used in the typical Boundary Waters cruising canoe. This length is short enough for high-cadence stroking and long enough for leverage in the turns.

Your straight paddle should be about two inches longer than your bent paddle. Long torsos and high seats require slightly longer paddles; short torsos and low seats suggest shorter paddles. Scientific formulas aside, a 54-inch bent-shaft and 56-inch straight paddle will get you around in fine style. Wide, sharp-cornered paddle blades are noisy and difficult to control, so choose a blade that is 7 to 8 inches wide (no wider!) and has well-rounded corners. If you prefer a very quiet paddle for fishing and approaching wildlife, consider a traditional "beavertail."

Ultralight Carbon Fiber Paddles

The lighter the paddle, the better! Good wood paddles weigh eighteen to twenty-four ounces—a half-pound lighter than most hardware store sticks. But if you think that's light, check out the ultralight, carbon-fiber bent blades that weigh eight to fourteen ounces! I'd feel undressed on any canoe trip without my ten-ounce graphite Zaveral paddle.

Paddling and Portaging Your Canoe

Paddling Your Canoe

If you can stroke forward and back and know how to "rudder," you can probably get around okay in the Boundary Waters. However, a knowledge of these strokes will make your canoe trip much more enjoyable.

Hut! Stroke or "Minnesota Switch" (Figure 7-1)

The easiest way to keep a canoe on course is to call HUT! (or whatever) and change paddle sides in unison with your partner. The technique was introduced by Minnesota canoe racers over fifty years ago and it remains the fastest way to paddle a canoe. Minnesota racers commonly change paddle sides every six to eight strokes or whenever the canoe wavers off course. Use the "Minnesota Switch" when paddling into a strong head wind.

Pitch Stroke (Figure 7-2)

The stern paddler uses the "pitch" stroke to keep the canoe from veering away from his or her paddling side. The pitch stroke is similar to, but more effi-

Figure 7-1. "The Minnesota Switch" or "HUT!" stroke.

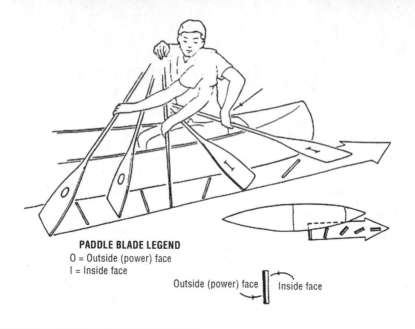

PADDLE BLADE LEGEND
O = Outside (power) face
I = Inside face

Outside (power) face | | Inside face

Figure 7-2. Pitch stroke.

cient and relaxing than, the popular J-stroke. Procedure: Turn the thumb of your top (grip) hand progressively *away* from your body as you pull the paddle through the water. Continue "pitching" the blade until your thumb points *straight down* and the face of the blade is parallel to the canoe. If the craft continues to veer away from your paddling side, push the paddle blade slightly outward.

Canadian Stroke (Figure 7-3)

The "Canadian" stroke is used by the stern paddler to keep the canoe on course. It is less powerful but more relaxing and quieter than the pitch and J-strokes. Procedure: Pitch the blade less severely than illustrated in Figure 7-2. Your top (grip) thumb will point about forty-five degrees to the water—rather than straight down—when the blade is at point (a). Finish by pushing the paddle outward in a wide arc, rear edge of the blade raised at a slight climbing angle to the water. The long outward "drag" on the climbing edge of the blade keeps the canoe on course. The Canadian stroke is best done with a long, narrow-bladed, straight paddle.

Silent, Underwater Stroke (Figure 7-4)

Use this quiet stroke in the bow or stern for fishing and approaching

A

Begin with
a J-stroke

Paddle
remains in
water as it
comes
forward

Figure 7-3. Canadian stroke.

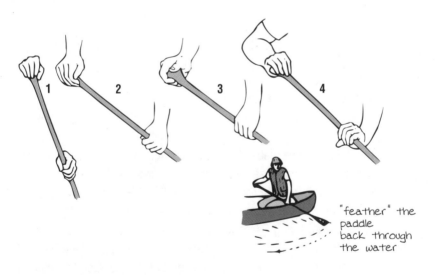

1 2 3 4

"feather" the
paddle
back through
the water

Figure 7-4. Silent, underwater stroke.

wildlife. Procedure: As you complete a "Canadian" stroke in the stern, or a "forward" stroke in the bow, turn your top (grip) hand 180 degrees and roll the paddle out and under the canoe for another stroke. The blade remains

Figure 7-5. Sweep strokes.

completely submerged throughout the stroke. You cannot do this stroke with a bent-shaft paddle.

Sweep Strokes (Figure 7-5)

Use the sweeps to turn the canoe in a wide arc, either toward or away from your paddling side.

Sculling Draw (Figure 7-6)

This impressive looking stroke will powerfully and quietly turn your canoe in any direction you want to go. It is most useful in shallow water where you can't submerge the whole paddle blade. Change the direction of the "scull" and the canoe follows suit. Europeans use a form of the sculling draw to propel their luxurious paddle boats through the canals of Venice. Procedure: Place the paddle in the water at a comfortable distance from the canoe. The paddle shaft may be at any angle to the water, though near vertical provides the most power. Now, turn the paddle blade forty-five degrees to the canoe and pull the paddle through the water about 2 feet. Then, reverse the leading edge of the blade and pull the paddle back to its starting point. The canoe will scoot toward your paddle.

To scull backward, apply power to the *back* side of the blade as you move it back and forth. The canoe will move smartly *away* from your paddle!

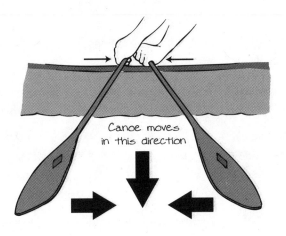

Canoe moves
in this direction

Figure 7-6. Sculling draw.

Big Water Tactics

Loading the Canoe

Most canoes handle better when loaded dead level. If an uneven distribution of weight is unavoidable, the lesser of two evils is to slightly lighten the bow. But a light bow will tend to weather-vane around in a head wind, making it difficult to keep the canoe on an upwind course. On the other hand, a weighted stern will provide better directional control in a following sea, though if the tail is too low, huge waves may pour in!

Unfortunately, retrimming your canoe to meet the changing whims of nature is practical only if there's room in the craft to move gear around. If there's not—and there won't be if you're carrying a passenger or are heavily packed for a long trip—you'd best adopt a "level trim" attitude and make the best of it. Be sure to keep the weight close to the center and low in the canoe.

When a canoe is paddled hard, the bow rises and the stern sinks into the hollow created by the wake, effectively knocking the boat out of trim and slowing its speed. The solution is to retrim the canoe by shifting the weight of the paddlers or cargo forward—simple enough if the craft has a sliding bow seat (essential on a serious Boundary Waters cruiser) or packs that can be shoved ahead.

With these thoughts in mind, let's review the "trim rules."

Trim Rules

1. Trim the canoe dead level for casual cruising. Keep gear centered and low in the canoe.

2. Trim the canoe slightly (one inch is enough) stern down in a strong tail wind.

3. Trim the canoe slightly bow down when paddling into a strong head wind. Be aware that you may have to lighten both ends of the canoe and revert to level trim if the waves are so large they come in over the bow or stern!

4. Trim the canoe slightly bow down for racing. Remember, when you push a canoe hard, the bow rises and the stern falls into the trough created by the wake.

Some paddlers glue a small "fish-eye" bubble level into the hull so they can see at a glance how their boat is running. It's easier to pour a cup of water into the boat and observe the flow. It should pool below the center thwart for casual cruising, a bit forward when you want to make time. Keep your eye on the puddle as you paddle and you'll learn a lot about the effects of hull speed on trim.

Positions for Running Upwind and Down

On the seat or on your knees, buttocks planted firmly against the leading edge of the seat frame, is the rule, in both tandem and solo canoes. The exception is when the lake "stands on edge"!

Here's a typical scenario. You're a quarter mile from shore when suddenly the wind blows up on the big lake. You point the bow upwind and paddle for dear life. Three hundred yards ahead is an island refuge. As you pour on the coal, waves pour determinedly over the bow. What to do? If the stern paddler stays put and the bow paddler moves behind the front seat, the bow will be lightened and the craft will rise more easily to the waves. However, the heavy stern may cause the craft to weather-vane, broach, and capsize.

The solution to this dilemma is for the stern paddler to shuffle forward, chest touching the stern thwart. He or she holds the paddle in a tight, deep rudder position and then commands the bow person to move quickly back behind the front seat. The weight shift lightens *both* ends of the canoe, and allows the craft to "teeter-totter" over the waves. Dead level trim is restored so there is no loss of directional control.

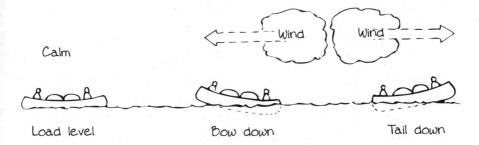

Calm

Load level   Bow down   Tail down

Tip: To check trim, pour some water into the canoe and see which way it flows.

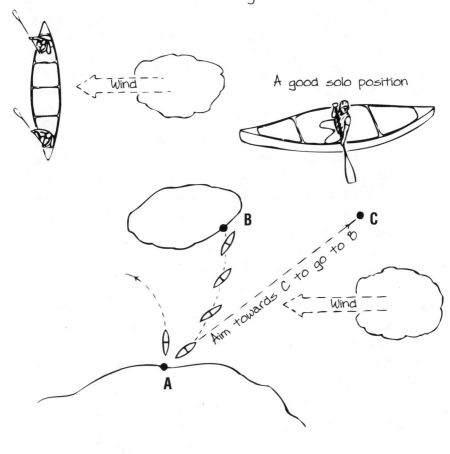

A good solo position

Aim towards C to go to B

Figure 7-7. Tacking.

Some canoeing experts advise paddlers to stay in their original positions on their seats or knees and simply "quarter" big waves at approximately a thirty-degree angle as the bow beats upwind. This procedure shortens the canoe's waterline and makes it easier for the craft to fit between waves. The result is that the canoe runs drier and rises more easily to the waves.

However, a canoe on a quartering tack is constantly on the edge of broaching to the wind. The stern paddler must have complete control of the craft. An error and over you go! That's why quartering waves is best reserved for experts. Beginners are best advised to move closer amidships, as suggested above, and paddle head on into the wind!

Going downwind in a light wind is great fun, more so if you scroll a small tarp around two paddles and use it as a makeshift sail. The problem surfaces when the wind strengthens and the canoe begins to surf. If the craft stalls on the crest of a wave, get set to swim! When suddenly the canoe feels lightheaded, act fast. The bow person should pour on the coal while the stern paddler holds a tight, deep rudder. Seconds later, the wave will pass and the canoe will slide into the trough of a smaller, more manageable wave. Now, "give 'er the ash" and get to shore before the scenario is repeated!

It Can Be Safe to Run Sideways in Big Waves

How well canoes run big waves is more a function of wave length than wave size. If you have a 17-foot canoe and the waves are spaced 12 feet apart, you're in for a very wet ride. Now, "quartering" must come into play or you'll fill with water and swamp. If "head-on" running (try this first) is out of the question and you can't hold a quartering course, give this a try as a last resort. When the nose descends into a wave trough, quickly turn the canoe broadside to the wave and brace your paddles deep in the water. Lean the canoe slightly away from the oncoming waves to keep out splash—and stay on those paddle braces! Your canoe now fits between the waves; it should bob like a cork, up one wave face, down another. If you keep a cool head, you'll blow safely to shore without swamping or capsizing.

Try it on a nice sunny day and you'll discover that running across the waves is mostly a matter of balance. Pretend you're riding a horse and you'll have a good time.

Make Your Open Water Crossings Short and Fast

Plan to stop and rest at a wind-protected spot every fifteen to thirty minutes. I study the map before I make a crossing and identify a safe haven. Then, I point her into the waves and push hard to get there as fast as possible. I figure on making about 1 mile an hour in a heavy head wind and 5 in a tail wind. Thus, I question any head-wind run of over half a mile, or 5 miles, if the wind is at my back. Those who have paddled with me will smile when they read this because they know I don't always follow my own advice.

Tacking

You're located at (A) on Figure 7-7. There's a great campsite at (B). Head toward it and the wind will blow you past your objective. What to do? Aim toward (C) and the wind will take you where you want to go. One Boundary Waters canoe trip will make you a "master tacker"!

Paddling on the Same Side

Canoeing texts are usually adamant that partners should never paddle on the same side of the canoe. Hogwash! Paddling on the same side—*in unison*—is the right medicine when you can't hold the canoe on course in a quartering or wide wind. Stroke together, stay centered on your seats (or kneel!) and you won't capsize. If the wind grows too strong for this tactic, the bow person should paddle *hard* while the stern person alternately paddles and rudders.

Let's review the rules for paddling big water:

1. Trim tail down in tail winds, bow down in head winds. Lighten both ends if things get dicey.

2. Use the wind and tack to distant points.

3. Don't lollygag when the wind is up. Pour on the coal and get to a safe haven as fast as you can.

4. Only canoeists who know canoeing should quarter into big waves. Beginners are best advised to paddle straight into them or wait ashore till the weather improves.

5. In a strong side wind, both partners may need to paddle on the same side of the canoe—or, the stern paddler may have to rudder while the bow powers ahead.

6. Being sideways to big waves can be a good plan if you learn to "roll with the punches."

Respect big water but don't fear it. A well-paddled canoe is incredibly seaworthy if you and your partner take the above suggestions to heart.

Paddling Alone

Tandem canoes are generally too big to be competently handled alone. If you're serious about "soloing," you'll want a properly sized, pure-bred solo canoe. My book *The Basic Essentials of Solo Canoeing* will get you started.

If you insist on soloing a tandem canoe on calm water, *kneel* at or just behind the yoke (you'll want knee pads!). Move a foot or two forward (bow trimmed slightly down) when paddling into a head wind. Kneel behind the yoke when running before a breeze.

Most tandem canoes are too wide at the center to allow a comfortable paddling stroke, so you way want to scoot sideways and place both knees close together in the bilge of the canoe. This "Canadian" position is very comfortable on quiet water, though it necessarily requires that you paddle on just one side.

All other "solo techniques"—paddling backward from the bow seat, or stroking in the stern with the bow weighted, are inefficient and, to a greater or lesser extent, downright dangerous!

Canoeing with a Passenger

One hundred fifty pounds of potatoes is a gentler, more predictable load than an equivalent weight of human cargo. Heavy packs don't move around in canoes! Passengers do, and as such, they don't exactly enhance the canoeing experience. Place a third adult or two small children in the belly of your canoe and it will ride lower, paddle harder, turn more slowly, and suffer more damage when you hit rocks. Loading and unloading gear will also take on new dimensions as you stall on shallow rocks or muck yards from the portage landing. On a happy note, three adults probably won't need to make a second trip over the portages!

Where to put your passenger(s) and gear is a problem. After years of canoe tripping with passengers of all sizes and ages, I've come to prefer the following arrangement for an adult or teenage passenger (**Figure 7-8**):

1. Set a large pack against the stern thwart to provide a soft backrest for your passenger. If the pack is very tall, place it on its side so it won't raise the center of gravity of the canoe too high.

2. Your passenger's legs could be pinned between packs and the yoke bar if the canoe capsizes. For this reason—and your passenger's comfort—you should remove the yoke from the canoe. **Figure 6-2** shows one way to make a quickly detachable carrying yoke.

Three people in a canoe

Stern

Bow

Passenger

Remove Yoke for comfort
and safety of passengers

Two kids

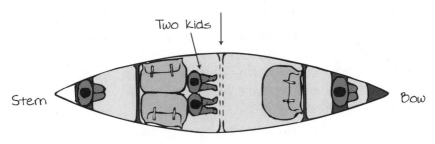

Stern

Bow

Plan A - Two adults and two children

Plan B - Two adults an two children

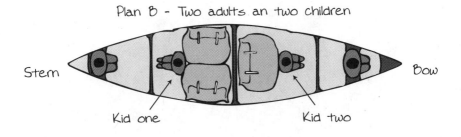

Stern

Bow

Kid one

Kid two

Figure 7-8. Packing strategies for different amounts of passengers and gear.

3. Additional packs are best placed side by side just behind the bow thwart. A thick "boat cushion" (life preserver) will keep your passenger's duff out of the accumulated bilge water. Generally, it's best if your passenger *does not* help paddle the canoe. Movable cargo, remember? The exception is when grinding into a steady head wind, where every stroke counts!

If your passenger is a small child, use the same procedure as above, except substitute a generously sized closed-cell foam sleeping pad for the boat cushion. If you have two small children, you have a problem: Place them side by side and they'll fight constantly. Separate them—one forward, one behind the yoke—and there's no place to put gear. **Figure 7-8** shows some less than perfect arrangements.

Portaging Your Canoe

Some people find that the hardest part about portaging a canoe is lifting it onto their shoulders. After years of canoeing with teenagers, I've come to prefer this energy-saving method: Both partners stand together on the left (port) side of the canoe, as illustrated in **Figure 7-9**. The "portager" stands *forward* of the yoke; his or her helper stands behind it.

1. Together, the partners raise the canoe on its side.

2. Both partners grasp the yoke and pull the canoe to their thighs (A).

3. Next, they transfer their left hand to the far (right) gunnel. Then, they transfer their right hand to the near gunnel. Note that both of the

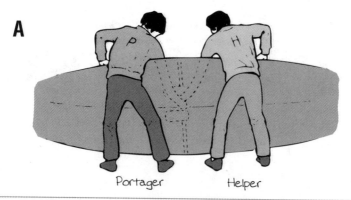

Figure 7-9. The two-person method of pulling a canoe into portage position.

B

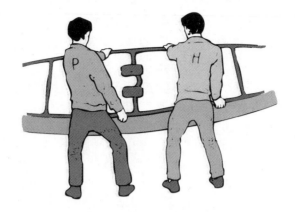

C

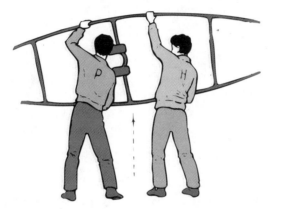

D

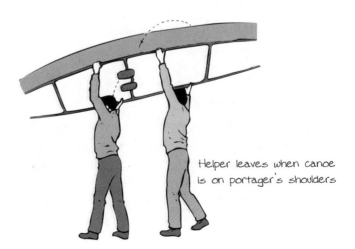

Helper leaves when canoe
is on portager's shoulders

portager's hands are forward of the yoke, while the helper's hands are behind it (B).

4. On signal, the canoe is raised overhead. The helper gets out of the way as the craft settles onto the portager's shoulders (C and D). Setting the canoe down is the reverse of picking it up.

If you canoe alone, you'll want to learn the "one person pickup." It is identical to the "two person" method, except that the portager stands at the center (yoke) of the canoe and, in step 4 above, his or her right hand grasps the near (left) gunnel just *behind* the yoke.

There is also the classic "end" lift, in which the canoe is rolled on end and raised overhead. I don't like this method: It grinds the end of the canoe into the ground!

Over the Portage and Through the Woods!

Once at the portage the fun begins. All your packs, paddles, life jackets, and sundries will have to be carried overland to the next lake. If you pack in *odd* units (one pack or three—never two or four) and follow this procedure, things will go much smoother.

1. Land the canoe parallel to shore if the topography permits.

2. One person holds the canoe while the other quickly strips it of gear. As soon as the craft is emptied, it is drawn up on land and placed well away from the traffic zone of the portage trail.

3. Each partner shoulders a pack and grabs a canoe paddle. Life vests are nested "coat-like" over packs, zipped around canoe thwarts, or shoved under pack flaps. Paddles, cameras, and binoculars are the only items that should be hand carried. Everything else should be secured inside a pack, or "stacked" and carried with the aid of a tumpline, as suggested in the next chapter!

If you and your partner have just one pack between you, the portage may be completed in a single carry. Two trips will be needed if you have three packs. First trip over the portage, each person carries a pack and paddle. The canoe and remaining pack are brought over on the second run. The canoe is the heaviest load, so you may want to carry it first—a good idea only if you *know the trail by heart!* If you don't, you'd best bring the packs first and scout the way.

Forest Service workers do their best to keep portages clear, but they have limited resources. Don't be surprised if you find storm-downed trees along seldom used trails. During high water times, normally impassable streams which are bypassed by portages may be easily canoeable. You won't spot deadfalls or a shortcut to the next lake if your head is buried under the yoke of a canoe!

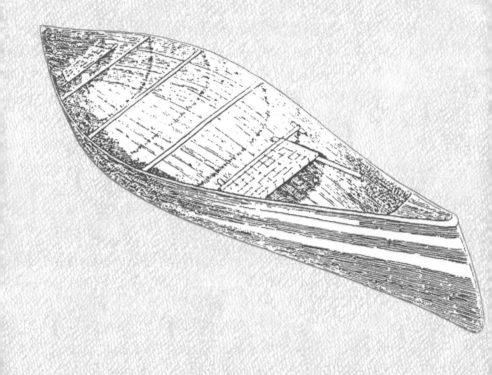

The Right Stuff—

Everything You Need To Know about Equipment

What you need in the way of equipment depends entirely on your traveling style. If portages are easy or nonexistent, whatever you can cram into your canoe is fair game. I've seen lawn chairs, cast iron Dutch ovens, and huge umbrella tents in the Boundary Waters. Once, I observed a galvanized garbage can in the belly of a canoe, which, the owners proudly asserted, was a bear-proof food cache!

At the other extreme are a minority of experienced travelers who are willing to make long, grueling portages to get away from the crowd. Some of these people pack so light that they sacrifice their own safety and comfort!

For example, the typical four-person tent weighs about three pounds more than a similar two-person model, but it provides nearly twice the space. That's something to consider when bad weather confines you to its fabric walls! Similarly, it makes no sense to omit a compact folding saw and hand axe if you rely solely on fires for all your cooking.

With experience comes wisdom. Paddlers who return to the Boundary Waters year after year ultimately adopt a mature, middle-of-the-road approach—they bring exactly what they need and no more! Sixty-five pounds per person (not including the canoe) is a reasonable weight for a week's load of food and camping gear. You can probably shave another ten pounds off this figure by tripling your equipment costs and using the latest high-tech gear.

Surprisingly, bulk is more important than weight. Most portages in the Boundary Waters are short, so a few additional pounds seldom matter. What does matter are loose items that won't fit inside packsacks. Herein lies the first rule of packing right:

Except for life vests, cameras, fishing rods, and paddles, everything must fit inside your packs!

Appendix 1 details what two people need for a week-long stay in the Boundary Waters. Here are some things to consider as you assemble your kit.

Packs

Until recently, canvas Duluth packs (**Figure 8-1**) have reigned supreme in the Boundary Waters. Now, a plethora of nylon hiking packs threatens to dethrone the king. For most canoeists, it's a love-hate relationship. Either they swear by Duluth packs or they swear at them. Nonetheless, traditional Duluth models remain popular with experienced canoeists because they are rugged, practical, relatively inexpensive, and easy to repair in the field. They are also as comfortable to carry as the best modern packs, *if* you use a tumpline!

Tumplines

A tumpline is a wide strap that attaches to a pack or bundle. You place this strap just above your forehead, lean forward into the trace, and take off down the trail. The early voyageurs carried hundreds of pounds with this rig, often stacking bundles a yard high over their heads. You may follow the lead of these historic

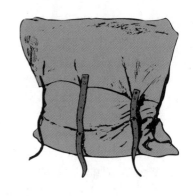

Figure 8-1. The Duluth Pack.

canoe men by placing awkward bundles, like day packs, paddles, and fishing rods, under the tump strap in the hollow of your back, as illustrated in **Figure 8-2.** When your neck and head begin to ache, cast off the tumpline and shift the load to the shoulder straps. Change back to the head strap when the pain is gone.

The key to comfortable packing is *keeping the load tight against your back*—easy enough when you're hiking on the flats or downhill. But ascend a steep grade and gravity will tear at your pack and threaten to bowl you over backward. Contoured pack frames and padded hip belts help stabilize the load, but only a tumpline anchors it tight against your back. The advantages of a tumpline on uphill grades are so pronounced that I urge you to try this simple experiment (**Figure 8-3**). Carry a heavy backpack up a steep staircase using the shoulder straps alone, then add a makeshift tumpline and repeat the procedure. Be sure you attach the tumpline *below* the point where the shoulder straps are sewn to the pack. You'll have to loosen the shoulder straps slightly to transfer the weight of the pack to the tumpline.

Remember to take the time to adjust the tumpline right! What works for one voyageur is wrong for another. If you're having trouble, try adjusting the tumpline before you give up on a grand idea.

Double-Packing

You're halfway through a two-week canoe trip and one of your heavy food packs is nearly exhausted. With judicious repacking, you can pare the load to just two packs. Your partner says he's willing to haul them both at once, if you'll manage the canoe. The payoff is that you won't have to make two trips over every portage. Should you buy the proposition?

Admittedly, you will save time by double-packing. But unless you're an old hand at it, you can trip and fall. The safest way to double-pack is to "stack-load" with the aid of a tumpline, as explained above. The dangerous alternative is to sling the extra pack across your chest, which obscures your feet and the trail ahead. Step wrong and you might twist an ankle; trip over a rock and you could break a leg!

I know Boundary Waters canoeists who have chest-packed for years without a single mishap. Others I know have been less fortunate. Indeed, turned ankles—which often result from double-packing—are the most common of all canoe country injuries!

Years ago, I asked my friend Bob Dannert to define a canoeing "expert." "Details!" said Bob. Small details, like watching every step you take, often spell the difference between a grand experi-

Figure 8-2. Packing with a tumpline.

Figure 8-3. Try this experiment to test your tumpline.

ence and a hurt you'll nurse for weeks.

If you must double-pack, "back-stack" your load, and use a tumpline. Only on the weeniest of portages should you carry a pack on your chest!

The alternative to double-packing or to making multiple trips over every portage is to stow everything in two packs—one heavy, one light. One partner carries the heavy pack, paddles, cameras, fishing gear, and PFDs (whew!), while the other brings the light pack and canoe. Another option is to place everything inside a single giant pack, like the huge #4 Duluth. However, big packs are awkward to handle and they don't stow well in a canoe. Either you lay them face down in soaking bilge water or you stand them precariously high against a thwart. Load an oversize pack into a tippy canoe while you're balanced on a slippery rock and you'll discover still another disadvantage.

Single carries are for Supermen and Wonderwomen! Mere mortals should keep pack weights and sizes reasonable. My advice? Select *three* moderately sized packs and place no more than fifty pounds of gear in each. Then adopt a hardened attitude about packing: "What doesn't fit doesn't go!"

Modern Canoe Packs

Modern packs that have spine-contoured shapes, padded hip belts, and adjustable sidewalls are a grand alternative to traditional Duluth styles. Indeed, sophisticated backpacks are almost essential if you carry heavy loads without the aid of a tumpline. Internal frames, hip belts, and other state-of-the-art backpacking features mimic, but don't equal the performance of tumplines on uphill grades, though they do provide greater control and comfort on the flats. Cooke Custom Sewing, Grade VI, Granite Gear, and Camp Trails (addresses in Appendix 2) all offer great packs for serious canoeists.

Before you commit to any pack, consider these points:

1. Portaging a quarter mile, three to six times a day (the typical BWCA scenario), is not the same as hiking 15 miles along a mountain trail. You don't need serious hiking gear for short carries. You do need equipment that stacks well in canoes!

2. Sophisticated packs offer little advantage over conventional Duluth packs if you use a tumpline. A tumpline that transfers the weight of the pack to your strong neck muscles replaces the value of hip belts, frames, and contoured shoulder straps. Tumplines also permit you to stack loose gear that won't fit inside your pack. Though "stacking" produces an awkward load that's unsuitable for serious hiking, it speeds progress on the short portages that characterize the Boundary Waters.

3. Sophisticated features don't come cheap. State-of-the-art backpacks cost nearly twice as much as traditional Duluth packs. A serious backpacker needs just one pack; a Boundary Waters canoeist needs three per canoe!

4. After a rain or capsize, you may have some wet, bulky gear that won't fit inside your pack. There's always room to "stuff one more thing" under the serviceably long closing flap of a classic Duluth pack.

5. The recommended #3 Duluth pack sits upright in the canoe, the pack mouth out of contact with bilge water. To load the pack into the canoe, you grab the pack by its "ears" (**Figure 8-4**) and, with a deft motion, swing it over the gunnels and plop it on the floor—no bending or stooping required. In contrast, a long-silhouette modern pack is too high to sit upright in a canoe. It must be placed belly down or sideways in the craft, with the pack mouth in the bilge water. This requires considerable bending and stooping—often dozens of times a day.

6. There's value in diversity. Why not have one Duluth pack, one modern pack, and a hard-shelled wanigan (dry box) for objects that may gouge your back? Naturally, I urge you to equip all your packs with tumplines.

Should You Equip Your Pack with a Hip Belt?

All the best hiking packs have padded hip belts that transfer part of the weight from your shoulders to your hips. Hip belts increase control on the flats

Figure 8-4. Loading a Duluth Pack.

and downhill grades, but they don't help on inclines. Hip belts also interfere with items you wear around your waist, such as a sheath knife or multi-pliers.

Hip belts don't fare well in canoes. They catch on thwarts and seats during loading operations and they remain submerged in bilge water and muck for long periods of time. Each time you portage you clip the dirty, dank strap around your waist. Whenever you set the pack down on a rotting cedar or the sharp granite of the Canadian shield, abrasion takes its toll. Eventually, the padding wears through.

Nonetheless, a hip belt is a decided advantage on long, grueling portages. By alternating between shoulder straps, hip belt, and tumpline, you can carry very heavy loads comfortably over difficult terrain. For this reason, veteran canoeists often equip their modern packs with hip belts *and* tumplines.

Rigid Packs

You'll want some sort of rigid dry box (wanigan) to store hard items like stoves, food, and cooking gear that might gouge your back. I prefer upright baskets for fragile items like eggs and optics, and side-loading boxes for hard gear like stoves and cookware. Why? Things slide around when wanigans are tipped up to portage. Top-loading baskets and boxes are never tipped.

Two of my favorite plastic wanigans are the Wanigan Canoe Pack & Pantry (formerly known as the "E. M. Wanigan"), available from Stormy Bay, and the new Hard Pack, made by Quetico Superior Canoe Packs.

Here are some other rigid containers you may want to consider:

1. Purchase a woven ash pack basket from L. L. Bean or Duluth Pack. Set the basket inside a waterproof plastic bag and nest this combo in a soft pack. Secure the mouth of the plastic bag with a loop of shock cord and you'll have a watertight seal. You can substitute a rectangular plastic trash can for the woven ash basket. You must cut off the rim of the can, however, or it will gouge your back.

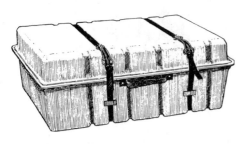

The late Calvin Rutstrum designed this outfit decades ago and it remains a good choice. I've worked with Duluth Pack to develop a special "Cruiser Combo"

Figure 8-5. The Wanigan Canoe Pack & Pantry.

packsack that accepts a standard, 18-inch-high pack basket. The "Cliff" model has a double canvas bottom, an extra long closing flap, and two large vertical side pockets. The shoulder straps and closing straps are made of leather.

Here's a tip. Insert a sheet of closed-cell foam between the back of the basket and the canvas pack material. Be sure the foam extends to the very bottom of the pack. You'll love the feel of the soft foam against your back when you portage.

2. Follow the lead of Canadian canoeists and place hard items in plastic olive jars or plastic barrels. Three or four 15-inch-diameter olive jars will fit in a #3 Duluth pack. Two-foot-high plastic barrels can be purchased from Western rafting companies. Marginally comfortable carrying harnesses are available from some Canadian outfitters.

3. Use a heavily varnished cardboard box instead of a pack basket or trash can. Duluth Pack continues to make their "Standard Food Pack," which accepts a traditional twenty-four-bottle beer carton.

Waterproof the Contents of Your Packs!

Your pack must be able to withstand an all-day rain or a capsize. This procedure will make any soft pack waterproof:

1. Insert a heavy (I recommend 6 mil) plastic bag into the pack. The bag should be nearly twice the length of the packsack to ensure a proper , seal. This is the waterproof liner.

You can order giant (54 x 33 inches) six-mil, flat plastic bags—or similar sized bags with a 6-inch side gusset (recommended!) from Superior Packs/CLG Enterprises, in Minneapolis. These incredibly strong, huge bags will fit the largest packs.

2. Nest a sturdy fabric bag (a second 6-mil plastic bag will do) inside the waterproof liner. This abrasion liner won't tear when you stuff gear into the pack. Note that the delicate waterproof liner is protectively sandwiched between two layers of tough material—the outside pack fabric and the inside abrasion liner. Use this "sandwich method" to protect everything you want to keep dry.

To waterproof your sleeping bag using the sandwich method, first stuff it into a nylon sack, which need not be waterproof. Then place this unit inside a strong plastic bag. This is your waterproof liner. Twist, fold over, and secure the waterproof liner with a loop of shock cord, then set the sealed bag into a slightly larger nylon stuff sack to protect it from abrasion.

Tent

It rains a lot in the BWCA so you better have a tent that keeps you dry! To check the foul-weather performance of any tent, pitch it on level ground and examine the fit of the rainfly (the sheet of waterproof nylon that covers the canopy). The fly should cover every seam and zipper! Exposed zippers or stitching *will* leak in prolonged rain no matter how well you seal them with seam sealant.

It won't take you long to discover that simple A-frame tents rank best in deterring rain, while domes, tipis, and other geometrically sophisticated tents with multi-seamed floors and sidewalls rank worst. Vestibules or alcoves, which provide space to store boots and wet gear, are worth the price in any weather. Tents like the popular Eureka Timberline, which are relatively "self-supporting" set up more easily on rock than traditional "U stake 'em" models.

Always use a plastic ground cloth *inside* your tent. The groundsheet will prevent pooled surface water that wicks through floor seams and worn floor fabric from soaking your sleeping bag. *Do not* place the plastic sheet under the tent as advised by some tent makers—rainwater may become trapped between it and the floor and be pressure-wicked by body weight into the sleeping compartment!

Cooking Tarp

Here's the scenario. It's supper time and raining heavily when you pull into camp. First order of business is to set up the tents and get out of the weather. If the rain persists, you'll skip supper and munch on granola bars. A hot meal can wait till morning. Right? Dead wrong!

Let's reprogram the scenario to read a bit differently. It's supper time and raining heavily when you pull into camp. First order of business is to erect the large rain tarp and get out of the weather. If possible, face the tarp toward your campfire, then formulate your battle plan. If you have a crew of four, two can pitch tents while one tends the fire and helps with supper. In no time, there will be soup and a cheery, protected place to share the joys of the day.

If you customize your tarp by adding extra loops and ties, (**Figure 8–6**)

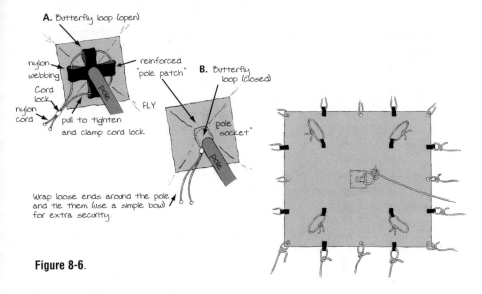

A. Butterfly loop (open)

nylon webbing
Cord lock
nylon cord

reinforced "pole patch"

B. Butterfly loop (closed)

FLY

Pole

pull to tighten and clamp cord lock

pole "socket"

Pole

Wrap loose ends around the pole and tie them (use a simple bow) for extra security.

Figure 8-6.

you'll be able to pitch it in a variety of ways. If you plan to use a center pole, add a butterfly "pole socket" in the fly center. The socket will keep the pole in place when the tarp is buffeted by wind. Fully customized tarps based on my plans are available from Cooke Custom Sewing of Lino Lakes, Minnesota.

The larger the tarp, the better! A tarp measuring 10 x 10 feet is about the right size for two. A 10 x 12 is better for four. If you have five to nine people, consider bringing two tarps! Chapter 10 suggests some slick ways to rig single and double tarps.

Don't bring cheap plastic tarps into the BWCA. They are heavy, bulky, stiff, and fragile. When they tear, they are often left behind to litter the wilderness. Frankly, I think the Forest Service should outlaw them!

Stove

Even if you prefer to cook on a campfire, you should bring a stove. Stoves simplify food preparation on rainy days, and are the only way to cook if dry conditions force the Forest Service to impose a "fire ban." Stoves that burn naphtha or unleaded gasoline are much more efficient than those that use propane, butane, or alcohol.

Gasoline is best stored in approved plastic containers or aluminum fuel bottles. Most stove problems are caused by varnishes that are released by old fuel left in stoves. So empty your stove tank (burn it dry!) after every canoe trip. Coleman and Blazo fuels are best used within six months after the cans are opened. You'll have fewer problems if you keep fuel containers full—the less air in the container, the slower the breakdown of the fuel.

Allow one gallon of gasoline per week for a party of four if you do all your cooking on a trail stove.

Chapter 9 details the cookware you need for canoeing the Boundary Waters.

Edged Tools

You need a *thin-bladed* knife, a folding saw, and a hand axe. Before you discount the hand axe, consider how you'll make fire when the woods are soaked with rain and the only wood available is a few well-drenched logs that you have no way to split! Chapter 10 shows how to use this much-maligned tool to make fire when rains come to stay.

Cutting line, slicing meats, chopping vegetables, and spreading jam and peanut butter are routine chores on canoe trips. A standard jackknife is adequate, but a thin-bladed (no more than ⅛ inch across the spine!) sheath knife, giant folder, or short fillet knife is more versatile. Reach deep into the peanut butter jar with your Swiss army knife and you'll instantly discover why you want a blade that's 4 to 5 inches long!

Good tool-steel knives sharpen more easily, take a keener edge, and are much less expensive than high-quality stainless models. They won't rust if you wipe them dry after every use and occasionally either slice greasy foods like cheese and salami or rub a little vegetable oil on the blade.

Clothing

Wool, acrylic, polypropylene, and polyester pile are the recommended fabrics for cool weather; cotton is fine for midsummer heat. Several thin garments, one layered over another, are warmer and more versatile than a single, heavy coat. Heavy wool socks, a light nylon wind shell, and a broad-brimmed hat are absolutely essential.

Summer temperatures in the BWCA can go from freezing, with wind chills near zero, to over 100 degrees F in a matter of days! Long underwear, a stocking cap, and gloves are important summer attire.

Rain Gear

A *two-piece* coated nylon rain suit or below-the-knee "fishermen's shirt" (called a *cagoule*) is essential. Size the jacket large enough to wear *over* your life vest. The pants should be wide and baggy so they'll slip easily over your boots.

Pant legs should not have cuffs, zippers, or elastic closures at the ankles. Zippers jam and break and they restrict ventilation. You'll find sturdy rainwear at discount stores and industrial supply centers.

Hats

I carry three hats—one for sun, one for rain, and a warm stocking cap. Your sun hat should have a broad brim or "desert neck flap" to protect your ears and neck. And speaking of sun, be sure to bring sunscreen, lip balm, and moisturizing lotion for your hands. Some people who have sensitive hands wear gloves when they paddle.

Footwear

Just about every type of footwear, from leather boots and sneakers to nylon "reef runners" and river sandals, can be seen in the Boundary Waters. And, depending on the weather and the nature of the trip, a good case can be made for every one. Indeed, the perfect shoes for canoeing have not yet been invented.

Arguments as to what shoes are best rage on, but when the smoke clears, experienced paddlers agree that the best choice is a sturdy pair of water-repellent calf-high boots for portaging, and a cool, breathable pair of lightweight shoes for camp. My personal preference for portaging and hiking is the L. L. Bean Maine Hunting Shoe with 12-inch-high leather tops and molded rubber bottoms. These "Bean Boots" are best worn with sheepskin, wool felt, or polyethylene insoles.

In camp, I switch to high-topped canvas sneakers. I also bring a light pair of nylon "reef runners" so I won't bruise my feet while swimming.

In late October, when the people and bugs are gone, friends and I take one last trip to the Boundary Waters. Daytime temperatures often hover around 40 degrees F. At night, the mercury frequently drops into the teens. More often than not, it rains and blows bloody murder; occasionally, it snows. On October 23, 1993, we encountered an inch of snow on one of the portage trails. That same day we broke quarter-inch-thick ice on a small stream that exited Cherokee Lake.

At this time of year, I wear sixteen-inch-high rubber boots with quarter inch thick neoprene insoles. In camp, I switch to flexible knee-high Tingley rubber overshoes with wool felt snowmobile liners.

My wardrobe includes wool/polyester long underwear, wool shirt, fleece sweater, and Thinsulate-filled Gore-Tex gloves. I bring a down jacket, a wool stocking cap, and a fleece neck warmer for chilly evenings around the campfire. The Boundary Waters is serious business when the snow falls!

Sleeping Gear

What you select depends on how classy you want to travel and how much money you want to spend. At the top of the list are expensive down bags, while at the bottom are discount store "gumbo-fill" specials that are no better than paired blankets. Frankly, a set of airy acrylic blankets, sandwiched "Boy Scout style," makes a perfectly good summer bed. A foam pad, like the deservedly popular Thermarest, will smooth the lumps and add considerable warmth to your sleeping system.

Make a full-length cotton case for your sleeping pad. The porous material will feel good against your skin on hot sweaty nights, and it will keep the slick nylon pad from sliding around in your tent as you sleep. A cover will also keep your pad clean and protect it from punctures.

Kids' Stuff

Most children love the Boundary Waters and the sense of freedom it brings. Kids are in awe of the beauty, the smells, the wildlife—and the quiet! Parents often report that their children are much more cooperative afield than at home.

Many parents are reluctant to take young children to the Boundary Waters, fearing they will catch cold, drown, die of hypothermia, or be eaten alive by bears. But kids are resilient. Neither rain nor cold, nor even an occasional capsize will deter them from having a good time, provided they are properly dressed and well fed.

Clothing for Kids

If you allow kids to wear blue jeans, cotton T-shirts, and cotton socks—their likely preference—they'll be miserable when it's cold and raining. And so will you! But dress them like little adults and your days will be filled with smiles.

Kids grow out of their clothes quickly, so it makes no sense to buy expensive outdoor clothing. On the other hand, they need the right stuff to be comfortable. What to do?

Inexpensive discount store acrylics are ideal for children. Acrylic garments are soft and warm, and they dry quickly after a rain. They are also tolerably cool on hot days. Choose acrylic shirts, stocking caps, gloves (the kind with the rubber dots on the palm), and sweaters.

Wool clothes may be too scratchy for some children, in which case you can substitute acrylics. However, a tightly woven wool shirt is worth bringing along. Wool repels water and insulates even when it's soaking wet. Few other fabrics feel as warm on a cold, rainy day. If you live in northern climes you'll find a wealth of serviceable wool shirts at area garage sales. Cook them in hot water for a while and they'll shrink to fit!

Polypropylene and pile are great for kids if you can find small sizes and good prices. Heat severely shrinks polypropylene and pile, and you can use this to your advantage to provide a custom fit. Use hot water—not your clothes dryer—to shrink-fit these garments. High dryer heat may actually melt polypropylene!

Rain Gear for Kids

The most practical and least expensive rain gear for children is a cut-to-fit plastic poncho, a standard raincoat, and a sou'wester hat with lined ear flaps. Here's the rationale: The youngster sits on a boat cushion in the middle of the canoe and wears all three garments. Arms that poke through the poncho sides stay dry, and the two-layer construction provides extra protection against blowing rain. The long draping sides of the poncho keep crossed legs and feet dry, while the sou'wester hat discourages dribbles at the neck. The outfit provides good ventilation when portaging.

Kids' Footwear

High-topped canvas basketball shoes are ideal for warm, dry days. Slip on inexpensive Tingley rubber boots when rains come to stay. *Two* pairs of socks should always be worn inside shoes. The thin, inner pair may be polypropylene, acrylic, or Thermax, while the outer pair should be nearly pure wool. The main reason for doubled socks is to prevent heat blisters, not to increase warmth. Inner socks should be worn *inside out*, so that blister-causing seams will be away from the skin.

Sleeping Bags and Kiddy Pads

A small acrylic blanket is adequate for summer travel in the Boundary Waters. The blanket will wash easily and dry quickly if your child has an "accident" while sleeping. Bring some diaper pins so you can convert the blanket to a sleeping bag on chilly nights. To this, add a closed-cell foam pad (carpet padding will suffice) for warmth below, and your child is set for the sandman.

Toys and Entertainment

Be sure to provide a downsized paddle and a small day pack for your little passenger. A favorite stuffed animal is sure to go along, so be sure to provide a "raincoat" (plastic poly bag) for it. Granola and homemade cookies are wholesome between-meal snacks, and they have no wrappers to pollute the environment—a concern when traveling with children, who unthinkingly throw things about.

Some campers bring along card and board games to keep children occupied on dreary days. I think books are a better idea. One of my most memorable times was when my girls were six and eight and our family was confined to our tent during a bad storm. My wife read Robert Service poems by candle lantern well into the night.

There is no need for entertainment when the sun returns again. The Boundary Waters is a wonderland and inquisitive youngsters will find plenty to do without nagging directions from their parents. There are great lessons to be learned from wild places. Parents should step aside and protectively allow their kids to experiment.

Packing Your Packs

Follow this procedure and you'll never have to eat damp oatmeal!

Distribute your food among several packs. This equalizes weight and provides a backup in the event you lose a pack to a hungry bear (more on this in Chapter 10). Double-seal your food in plastic, as suggested in Chapter 9, and place meals in the *bottom* one-fourth of each pack. Pack everything in *horizontal* layers so the back of your packsack will follow the curve of your spine. You may want to pack things in this order:

First, set your sleeping bag on top of the food packets.

Your foam sleeping pad goes in next, followed by your clothes, which are contained in a pillowcase-size, nylon stuff sack. Put your remaining sundries on top of your clothes bag.

Now, roll down and seal the inner abrasion liner. The tent goes on top. It should fit snugly, like a cork in a bottle. Stakes and poles are best packed in a separate bag!

When you're satisfied with the arrangement, roll down and seal the outer, waterproof pack liner. Place your rain gear and tent pole bag on top. Sew nylon loops to the pole bag ends and run the closing straps of the pack flap through the loops so poles won't slide out from under the pack flap.

Note that everything is contained and watertight. The tent, which may be wet or damp, is protected from a capsize, and is isolated from your dry clothing and sleeping gear. Long tent poles that won't fit crossways in your pack won't head for the deep six if you capsize.

In camp, unpacking is easy. Rain gear, tent, and poles are right on top of your pack, followed by sundries, clothes, and sleeping gear. Food stays put until you need it.

Packing the Canoe

Adopt a standard procedure for packing and unpacking your canoe. Your system should be geared for speed and "level trim." **Figure 8-6** shows some common packing layouts.

Locate packs so that rain gear, nylon wind shell, gloves, and sweater are handy. Your canoe will rise to the waves more easily if you keep weight close to the center of the canoe. Don't "string out" gear or pile it high above the gunnels.

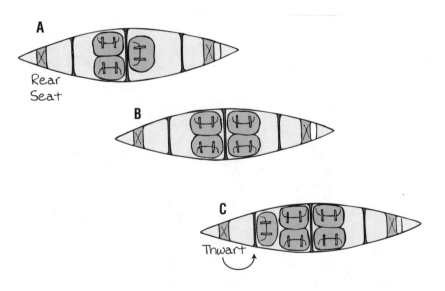

Figure 8-7. Some common packing arrangements.

Fast Fixin's—Easy Ways To Prepare Great Trail Meals!

In 1967, a friend and I loaded my new Sawyer Cruiser canoe atop his station wagon and headed north to Grand Marais, Minnesota—gateway to the BWCA. Our trip lasted ten days and traversed 100 miles—fairly substantial for first-timers. We began on Seagull Lake, swung north almost to Ely, then followed the Canadian border east to Trail's End landing on Saganaga Lake. By today's standards, we were marginally prepared. Our primitive single-walled nylon tent leaked in the sporadic rains, our little Sawyer canoe swamped in waves, and our bland but nutritious meals took too long to prepare. Nonetheless, we had a marvelous time.

Other than instant soups and the famed Boy Scout trail packs, dried foods were largely a novelty in the 1960s. It took know-how and experience to assemble well-balanced lightweight meals, so my friend and I decided that it would be best if an experienced outfitter supplied our food. Both of us were serious coffee drinkers, and we strongly noted this on the menu request form.

"No problem," assured our outfitter. "It'll all be packed and waiting when you arrive at our base in Grand Marais."

Disappointment reared its head at supper time the first night out, when we discovered that one pint of ground coffee would have to last ten days. My friend was even more furious when he learned that there was no cream or sugar. In place of what we needed were things we didn't want—white bread for sandwiches and French toast, hot chocolate, and instant pistachio pudding. We vowed that next year we'd do our own food planning!

Dried foods have come a long way since the 1960s. Now, you can get almost anything from cholesterol-free egg substitutes to sour cream at big league supermarkets and cooperatives. What you can't find in local stores you can get by mail-order from specialty houses. Hamburger, beans, beef jerky, and other staples can be easily dehydrated and vacuum sealed at home (more on this later). And if this seems like too much work, canoe outfitters will wow you with a variety of delicious freeze-dried offerings, from filet mignon to lobster Biscayne.

However, there's satisfaction in self-sufficiency. If you love good food, you'll want to provide for your own tastes. Here's how to prepare good meals without a lot of work.

Hardware

For a party of four, you'll need one 10-inch-diameter, Teflon-coated skillet with cover, two *nesting* pots with covers, and a twelve-cup coffee pot or teakettle. The largest pot should have a sixteen-cup capacity so you can cook pasta without gluing it to the bottom. Pots may be aluminum, stainless steel, or porcelain-lined steel.

You'll be cooking on a trail stove or Forest Service grill so wire bail handles are not essential. One long pot handle or two protruding metal "ears" per pot are adequate if you have insulated pot holders—gloves, bandannas, or pliers. Discount store kitchenware often works better than expensive pots and pans that are designed for camping. This is especially true for skillets.

I purchase a high-grade Teflon-lined skillet and replace the Bakelite handle with a quickly removable one that I made from 0.187-inch-diameter spring wire (see **Figure 9-1**). The mounting bracket for the handle is made from hardware store aluminum flat stock. It secures with two brass bolts that are easily detached when the pan wears out. I also outfit some of my pots with these rigid wire handles. I recently encouraged Kevin Carr of Chosen Valley Canoe Accessories to manufacture a universal handle kit like the one described. The "CVCA" kit contains two spring wire handles, plus two mounting brackets and four bolts. You drill holes and bolt on the bracket—a five-minute job. See Appendix 2 for CVCA address and e-mail information.

A couple of tips on camping cookware. Engrave lines on the pot sides at two-cup intervals and write the total capacity (e.g., sixteen cups) just below the rim. This will eliminate guesswork and the need for measuring cups at meal time. For faster heating, you may want to blacken the bottoms of your aluminum pots. Alumablack—a product used for blackening aluminum hardware

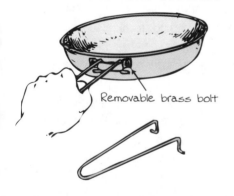

Commercial Teflon™-lined skillet

Removable brass bolt

Figure 9-1. Converted skillet.

Figure 9-2. Two methods of cooking, a Dutch oven (A) and a Reflector Oven (B).

on firearms—is ideal for this purpose. Every gun shop has it.

A wide-based teakettle heats faster and is less tippy than a coffee pot, and it permits you to pour with one hand. Pack fresh onions, green peppers, and other crushables inside your empty teakettle (see "Meal Management Tricks" in Chapter 9).

You may also want an oven. You can buy commercial models or simply rig a "double-pan" or Dutch oven from the cookware you already have. You can also prop a frying pan to face the fire and cook your bakestuff by reflected heat. **Figure 9-2** shows the traditional procedures.

Baking is a rather time-consuming process, one best reserved for lazy layover days. Pita, bagels, nutritious crackers, and an assortment of preservative-filled cocktail breads and cakes that keep for weeks have largely replaced the need for fresh baked goods. Nonetheless, if you enjoy baking, do it. After all, it's your canoe trip and you need to please no one but yourself!

Be sure to provide an insulated cup, sturdy plastic bowl, and a metal fork and spoon for each person. A stainless steel cup makes a handy ladle.

You may also want a fabric utensil roll that has snaps or ties at the top so you can hang it from a branch or overhead line. Contents should include a large wooden spoon, wire whip, rubber spatula, bamboo tongs, regulation cast aluminum Boy Scout pot gripper (these are the best!), Teflon-friendly wood or plastic pancake turner, and a removable spring-steel handle for your frying pan.

For dishwashing, bring a 3M nylon "scratcher," Teflon-safe nylon sponge, and a small bottle of biodegradable detergent. Pack a few sheets of paper toweling with every meal and you won't have to dry dirty cotton dish towels.

Spices

Dried foods are generally pretty bland unless they're heavily spiced. I carry oregano, garlic powder, seasoned salt, black pepper, and cayenne inside small film containers that are kept in a nylon "spice bag."

Packing the Kitchen

Nest the pots and covers and place them in a generously sized fabric bag. Pack spices, dishwashing materials, and your Sierra cup ladle inside the smallest pot, along with the nesting plastic bowls. Forks and spoons go inside the utensil roll. Everyone carries his or her own drinking cup in a thwart bag or on a lanyard, tied to the canoe. The teakettle or coffee pot is usually the last thing that's packed when you break camp in the morning. For this reason—and because you may want noontime tea or soup—it is best placed in a fabric bag and packed at the top of a pack, where you can get at it quickly.

Containers for Powders and Liquids

Sugar, flour, and other powdered foods may be safely carried in sealed plastic bags that are nested inside strong nylon or cotton bags. Use plastic bottles for cooking oil, pancake syrup, jam, and other liquids. Laboratory-proven Nalgene bottles are the most reliable field containers, but they are very expensive. Some hospitals and clinics still routinely discard strong plastic bottles that are used to store sterile, intravenous solutions. These containers are watertight, lightweight, and nearly indestructible. And they don't seem to hold food odors like other plastics. They come in graduated sizes from 500 to 1500 ml and have a convenient lanyard hole. Ask your doctor to save these IV bottles for you—they're being replaced in hospitals by plastic bags, so get a few while you still can.

Easy Breakfasts

Instant Quaker Oats or Cream of Wheat with raisins and beef jerky is the traditional fare for fast moving days when you want to "get up and go." Here are some flavorful options that require less than twenty minutes to prepare.

Cinnamon/Rice and Golden Raisins

When I was a kid, one of my favorite breakfasts consisted of hot milk, steamed white rice, golden raisins, and cinnamon and sugar to taste. I had forgotten how good this was until a friend prepared it on a recent Boundary Waters trip. In the old days, mom simmered long-grain rice in whole milk. Today, fast cooking Minute Rice and non-fat dry milk work almost as well. Kids and adults both relish this easy-to-prepare nutritious meal. Add powdered orange drink or dehydrated fruit and you'll have a balanced meal.

When Oatmeal Gets Boring, Try These Delicious Hot Cereals!

Red River Cereal is a nutritious blend of crunchy grains that's served in the best fishing camps in Canada. It cooks to a rich, creamy consistency in just five minutes.

Big Bill's Multi Grain Cereal is another tasty Canadian product. Sweetened malted whole milk provides a unique flavor.

Hot Ralston is another traditional alternative to oatmeal. Simmer raisins, dehydrated apples, cinnamon, and brown sugar for a few minutes in the boiling water *before* you add the cereal. (This works for Red River and Bill's, too.)

Tricks with Eggs

If space and weight are a concern, you'll want to carry freeze-dried eggs. Otherwise, fresh eggs are less expensive and tastier. Farm-fresh eggs will keep for weeks without refrigeration!

Small and medium size eggs have thicker shells than large eggs, so they're less apt to break on a canoe trip. I carry fresh eggs in their original cardboard (not Styrofoam!) containers. I seal each egg carton in a plastic poly bag then place it inside a strong Tupperware container that holds up to four dozen eggs. The Tupperware safe goes inside my pack basket or on top of my Duluth pack. I can't recall when I've ever had a spoiled or broken egg. The Tupperware box doubles as a dish pan, and as a convenient safe for other crushables when the eggs are gone.

Egg/Cheese McPita and McTortilla

Freshly baked pita bread and tortillas will keep at least two weeks on a midsummer canoe trip if they are well sealed when you leave home. They're a delicious and versatile food around camp.

Fry and set aside two thin slices of Canadian bacon or summer sausage per person. Scramble one egg per person and set it aside. Now, lightly fry an open-face Mediterranean pocket bread (pita) or a tortilla in a teaspoonful of cooking oil. When the bottom of the pita or tortilla is brown (about twenty seconds), flip the bread over and lay thinly sliced cheese on top. Pile on the bacon or sausage and egg, add a dash of your favorite salsa (optional), and immediately toss a dash of cold water into the sizzling skillet. Cover and steam for fifteen seconds then serve *immediately*. In less than a minute you'll have a wholesome, delicious sandwich everyone will enjoy. You can also fry the egg over easy, or even omit it entirely.

Garlic Cheese Pita or Garlic Cheese Burrito

Cut a pita bread in half and fill the pocket with thinly sliced or grated cheddar, Monterey jack, or Swiss cheese. Sprinkle garlic powder and oregano (optional) over the cheese. Fry each pita half in a well-oiled, covered skillet for about twenty seconds. Flip the pita, adding a dash of cold water to "steam the cheese," and cook covered for another fifteen seconds.

Tortillas are less filling that pitas but they have a more delicate toasty flavor. For a garlic cheese burrito, cook each tortilla flat in a well-oiled skillet for about ten seconds, then flip it over and add cheese and garlic powder to the toasted side. Immediately roll the tortilla into a burrito shape, add cold water to steam, then cover and simmer for twenty seconds. Mmmm, good! Serve "garlic cheese burritos" as an hors d'oeuvre with chili, pasta dishes, and soup.

Cinnamon Tortillas, Stewed Fruit, and Canadian Bacon

Make a tortilla burrito as described above, but substitute margarine, cinnamon, and white or brown sugar for the cheese and garlic. Tastes just like a cinnamon roll!

Boiled dehydrated apples and brown sugar, served with a side of Canadian bacon, round out this delightful breakfast.

Launching Lunch

Lunches should be easy. If you can't unwrap it, spread it, or slice it, forget it! Here again, pita bread is an important staple. Fill pitas with cheese, jam, peanut butter, and hard salami. For variety, substitute flavored Rye Krisp, Wheat Thins, and other crackers for pita bread, and serve granola, beef jerky, meat sticks, cookies, dehydrated fruit, and salted nut rolls. Lightweight Nutrasweet-flavored drink mixes make tepid water bearable.

I can't imagine lunch in the Boundary Waters without Hudson Bay Bread. This chewy, granola-style bar is traditional traveling fare in youth camps from Maine to Minnesota. Charles L. Sommers Canoe Base in Ely, Minnesota, has been serving it to Boy Scouts since 1960. Here's the official recipe, which has been modified (substantially improved!) by Brian Buhl, who was a Director of Programs at the Scout Base until 1999. This recipe provides a ten-day supply for four hungry teenagers.

Cream together three cups soft margarine or butter, four cups white sugar, one-third cup light Karo corn syrup, two-thirds cup honey, and two teaspoons of maple flavoring (Mapleine). Gradually add one and a half cups sliced almonds and one cup (or more!) chocolate chips. Some cooks (not Brian) also add shredded coconut and raisins. Now mix in nineteen cups finely ground rolled oats—*not* instant oats.

Press the mixture into a greased cake pan in a layer about ¼ to ½ inch thick. Bake at 325 degrees F for about twenty minutes, until golden brown. Don't overcook! Press down on the Hudson Bay bread with a spatula (to prevent crumbling) before you cut and remove the squares from the pan. "Scout serving size" (twice what most adults will tolerate) measures 3.5 inches square, so as to fit exactly in protective half-gallon milk cartons. I wrap each square in plastic wrap then vacuum seal each day's lunch supply. Shelf life is a full summer or more. Unused bars freeze well and keep till next year.

On into Supper

Pork chops, stroganoff, chicken Alfredo, Cajun black beans with rice, and spumoni ice cream are all available in freeze-dried form. You can even get freeze-dried steaks, if you can find them—and afford them!

Few campers are willing to pay the high prices that freeze-dried specialty foods command. As a result, there are fewer dried food makers today than a decade ago. The ones that survive eke a meager profit from selling traditional entrees like "spaghetti and meatballs," "beef stroganoff," and "Denver omelets" to inexperienced campers who lack the skills to produce similar meals from supermarket offerings.

Here are some things to consider as you plan your dehydrated suppers.

I. Most dried entrees consist of three parts—pasta or rice; freeze-dried/dehydrated chicken, beef, or shrimp; and spices. Remember this, and you can mix and match a variety of foods to suit your tastes.

2. The meat is by far the most expensive part of any dried meal. A quarter pound of freeze-dried hamburger (essential to make spaghetti, stroganoff, or chili) costs three times as much as a Big Mac! Chicken and shrimp are even more expensive.

However, you can easily dry these meats yourself in an inexpensive home dehydrator. Here's how to dehydrate hamburger:

1. Fry the hamburger and drain the grease. I allow cooked hamburger to stand in a wire strainer for several minutes, then I pour boiling water through the meat to remove as much fat as possible.

2. Line each dehydrator tray with a few sheets of absorbent paper toweling and spread the hamburger out on the trays. Allow no more than one pound (quarter-inch thickness) of hamburger per tray.

3. Turn the dehydrator to high (140 degrees F) and come back in twenty-four hours. Vacuum-seal[1] (preferably) the dried hamburger in one-pound lots, or double-bag it in Ziploc bags. Use a drinking straw to remove as much air as possible from the Ziploc bags. Vacuum-sealed, dehydrated hamburger will keep at least a year at room temperature; dehydrated hamburger that has been carefully stored in Ziploc bags should last a month. As a safety precaution, keep dehydrated meats frozen until just before your trip. Use dehydrated hamburger in spaghetti, chili, soups, and stews.

To prepare spaghetti, you'll need dehydrated hamburger, pasta, spices, and tomato sauce. To make the dehydrated spaghetti sauce, line the dehydrator trays with plastic cling wrap and spread the sauce evenly on the trays. In twelve hours you'll have a thin, rubbery mass that resembles a fruit roll-up. Peel the dried sauce off the plastic wrap, roll it up, and freeze it. Later, break chunks into a plastic poly bottle. Add water to the chunks to rehydrate the sauce.

If you don't want to mess with this foolishness, simply order tomato powder at your local co-op. Add a little water to the powder and you'll get paste; add more water, and you'll have sauce or soup.

Chili requires dehydrated beans, which are easily made from canned beans. Pour the liquid off the beans. Put the beans directly on the dehydrator tray and turn the heat to high. The beans will be dried and ready to pack in about eight hours.

---

[1] Several excellent vacuum sealing machines are available. I've had good luck with a powerful home unit called the Foodsaver. It's available from Nationwide Marketing, Inc. 1550 Bryant Street, Suite 850, San Francisco, CA 94103 (800) 777–5452.

Hamburger/Cheese/Vegetable Soup

Here's a hearty meal for four that takes just ten minutes to prepare:

Add one pound (about three-fourths cup) of dried hamburger to eight package servings of vegetable soup. Toss in a heavy handful of wide egg noodles or instant rice, and add some dried mushrooms (optional) and a few slices of cheese. A dash of red pepper and garlic powder complete the recipe. I'm betting this will be one of your favorite meals!

Pita Pizza

After several days of one-pot meals, you'll appreciate some solid food that you can chew. Everyone will love "pita pizza." You'll need one or two pieces of pita bread per person, dried tomato powder, fresh mozzarella cheese (hard, fresh cheese keeps nearly a month if it's encased in wax or vacuum sealed), oregano, garlic powder, salt, and cayenne pepper. You can also add pepperoni, summer sausage, hard salami, Canadian bacon, fresh onion, green pepper, or dried mushrooms.

Thin-slice and fry the meat and drain off the grease on paper toweling. Chop the vegetables, fry them in light oil, then drain off the grease and set them aside. Rehydrate the mushrooms in water for several minutes, then pour off the water, pat dry the mushrooms, and lightly fry them in oil. Set the mushrooms aside along with the other vegetables.

To make the pizza sauce, pour a half cup of tomato powder into a bowl and add water to make a thick paste. Sprinkle on oregano, garlic, salt, and cayenne. Allow the sauce to blend for a few minutes.

Fry an open-faced pita at low heat in a well-oiled, covered skillet. When the bottom of the pita is brown (about twenty seconds), flip the pita over and thickly spread on tomato sauce, cheese, meat, and vegetables to taste. Immediately add a dash of water (to steam-melt the cheese) and cover the pan. Allow the pizza to cook at very low heat for half a minute, or until the cheese has melted.

Meal Management Tricks

Add Fresh Vegetables to All Your "One-Pot" Meals!

Unrefrigerated onions, tomatoes, and green peppers will keep about five days on a canoe trip, if they are properly packed.

Onions are so tough you can just place them in a cotton or paper bag. Stow the bag inside a rigid container, like a covered teapot, cardboard milk carton, or plastic dry box.

Use the following procedure for green peppers and tomatoes, which spoil quickly and are easily bruised.

I. Wash the vegetables, then immerse them in a sink full of drinking water that has been treated with about one-eighth cup (the amount isn't critical) of chlorine bleach. Allow the vegetables to soak for several minutes in the treated water before you dry and pack them away. The bleach will kill the surface bacteria that promote spoilage. A similar procedure is used in some of America's finest restaurants to keep vegetables fresh.

You may use only a small portion of a tomato or pepper at each meal. Wash in fresh water only the portion you need. Do not wash the entire vegetable! Doing so will introduce waterborne bacteria which may precipitate spoilage.

2. Separately wrap each tomato or green pepper in clean paper toweling. Pack the towel-wrapped veggies in a paper or cotton sack and set the sack inside a crush-proof container, as suggested above. Do not wrap vegetables in non-porous plastic!

A squish-resistant, plastic "tennis ball" tube makes a good safe to store tomatoes or onions. Be sure to punch holes in the sides of the tube so air will circulate.

Packing Food in Color-Coded Stuff Sacks

Your crew will consume twenty-one meals on a seven-day canoe trip. That's a lot of food to keep track of. This procedure will simplify packing and help you identify who has what meal.

I. Lay out on the floor twenty-one large poly bags in three rows of seven each. Pack each group breakfast in a separate bag in the bottom row. Lunches go in the middle row of bags, suppers in the top row.

2. Seal each plastic bag and place it in a sturdy, color-coded nylon stuff sack. I pack breakfasts in "green" sacks, lunches in "blue," and suppers in "red." Tag the contents of each stuff sack so you can identify each meal.

Say your crew decides to prepare a spaghetti supper. How can you find it among the twenty-one meal bags? Easy! Suppers are packed in "red" bags, remember? Get out the seven red bags and look for the "spaghetti" label. What could be easier?

Tasty Cooking Tricks

Ever notice how some campers can always prepare great meals while others can't warm soup without burning it? Good camp chefs know a wealth of tasty cooking tricks. Here are a few that will speed food preparation and save fuel.

Make a Cozy Sweater for Your Cooking Pots!

It's a cold, blustery day and you're anxious for a hot meal. You place the pot of freeze-dried chili on your stove to heat, taking care to stir constantly so the food won't burn. You know that if you stop stirring and cover the pot, the chili will boil faster. However, it may also burn and stick to the pot bottom. On the other hand, if you continue to stir the uncovered food, heat will escape into the air and the chili will take much longer to cook. What to do?

Make an insulated sweater "cozy" for your pot from any quilted or knitted material. A two-piece cozy (top hat and pot band) like the one illustrated in **Figure 9-3** is more versatile and energy efficient than a one-piece model. Here's how to use your two-piece cozy.

1. Secure the insulated band around the pot before you begin cooking. Pour cold water into the pot and add only the dehydrated hamburger and vegetables. Tightly cover the pot and Velcro down the cozy skirt to provide an overlapping seal. Turn the stove to high and attend to other chores.

2. When the water boils, reduce the heat to "medium" and add the chili beans, tomato powder, and spices. Stir vigorously until the fixin's are blended and the water is boiling again (about thirty seconds).

3. Turn off the stove, put on the cover and cozy, and set the pot on a piece of closed-cell foam, a square of old carpeting, or a pot holder. The chili will "slow cook" to perfection in about twenty minutes!

The advantage of the two-piece cozy over a one-piece "teapot" model is that the wide band continues to insulate the pot sides when you remove the cover to stir. The skirted "top hat" can also be used alone on top of a skillet cover to increase its thermal efficiency. It is especially useful when steam-cooking pita pizza and burritos. Your pots may be insulated with spare clothing if you don't have a fitted cozy. But be careful: Nylon or acrylic fabrics will melt! Cotton or wool fabrics are best. I recently encouraged Quetico Superior Packs/CLG Enterprises to manufacture the insulated cozies I designed. They are called "Cliff

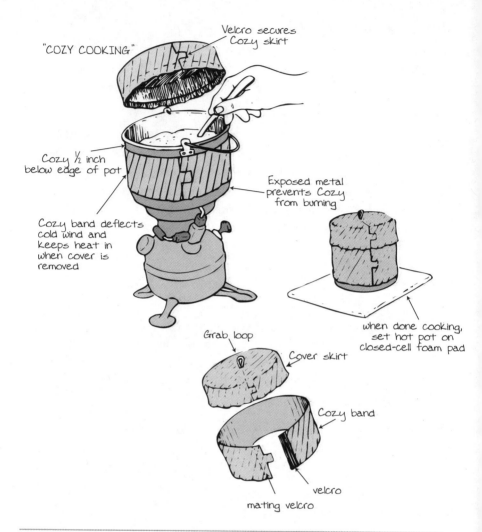

"COZY COOKING"

Velcro secures
Cozy skirt

Cozy ½ inch
below edge of pot

Exposed metal
prevents Cozy
from burning

Cozy band deflects
cold wind and
keeps heat in
when cover is
removed

when done cooking,
set hot pot on
closed-cell foam pad

Grab loop

Cover skirt

Cozy band

velcro

mating velcro

Figure 9-3. Cozy cooking.

cozies," and are constructed of thick wool fleece. Three sizes are available.
Contact Quetico Superior Packs (Appendix 2) for details. (I have no financial
arrangement with this company for using my design or my name. I recommend
"Cliff cozies" to you because they are an excellent product.)

As mentioned, a dash of cold water in a hot, covered skillet will quickly
steam-cook foods. You can also use this method to restore the freshness of week-
old bagels, pita bread, and tortillas. Simply "steam grill" the bread in a covered
skillet for a few seconds.

Finally, if you insist on carrying loaves of bread, here's an old woodsman's trick that guarantees perfect toast: Distribute a heavy pinch of table salt on the surface of a hot, dry (no grease!) skillet. Set a slice of bread on the salt. *Do not* cover! When the bottom of the bread is toasted to a golden brown, flip the bread over and toast the other side. The salt won't burn or stick to the bread or skillet.

10 A Bomb-Proof Canoe Camp!

Some years ago, after a dangerous storm with winds to 50 miles an hour, a teenager and I went out to fetch water on Little Saganaga Lake in the Boundary Waters Canoe Area. Everywhere, wind and rain had wreaked havoc upon the land. Clumps of uprooted vegetation floated aimlessly about and waist-thick trees were downed and scattered all around. We could see three other camps from our vantage point and there was not a tent or tarp standing in any one of them. One site revealed a thin column of smoke which suggested a barely sputtering blaze. There was not a whisper of flame in the others. A comically intricate network of ropes, pressured low by heavy piles of wet clothing was a universal phenomenon.

We filled our kettles with clean water then cruised on back to our campsite where five teenagers were busily tending to chores. Daintily strung from a line near the crackling fire was the only wet gear in camp—a red wool lumberjack shirt and some bathing suits and towels. Held firm by a web of brightly colored parachute cords (for good visibility in failing light), our two low-slung rain tarps had weathered the storm without pooling water. Everything beneath them was sunshine dry.

I pulled the canoe ashore and set the huge teapot on the fire, then turned to a sandy-haired girl nearby. "You guys stay dry last night?" I asked.

"Yeah, except my wool jacket, which dumbo here (pointing to her freckle-faced friend) borrowed and left out all night!"

"Don't fight, children," I teased. "We won't blow this place till noon. By then, everything will be dry. Now if you guys wanna see a show, check out our neighbors round the bend." "Yeah," perked the boy who had joined me in the canoe—"we got us one bomb-proof canoe camp here!"

Surprisingly, "bomb-proofing" a canoe camp against the cruelties of nature is more a function of skill than equipment. As the anecdote suggests, you don't have to paddle far to find campers with high-tech gear and no savvy. So first learn the ropes, then attend to equipment. And take the following suggestions seriously.

Tents and Tarps

Always Use a Waterproof Ground Cloth Inside Your Tent!

I mentioned this in the last chapter, but it's so important that it bears repeating here. The best rain tent won't keep you dry if it's pitched in a low spot—a situation you can't control on the federally designated tent sites in the Boundary Waters. Indeed, even high ground will soak through if it rains long enough and hard enough. It follows that you *absolutely, positively* must place a watertight plastic layer between your sleeping gear and the tent floor.

Check out a tent full of teenagers after a heavy rain: If there was no protective ground cloth, the kids who occupied the perimeter of the tent will be soaking wet. Those who slept in the middle will be comfortably dry and tight-lipped about the reason why!

Some canoeists place a second ground cloth under the floor of their tent to protect it from scrapes. Frankly, I think this is a bad idea. Here's why:

1. If it rains hard and long enough, water may become trapped between the exterior plastic and tent floor, and be pressure-wicked by body weight into the sleeping compartment. Using a ground cloth under the floor is akin to pitching your tent on a slab of concrete!

2. If it's storming when you pull into camp, you'll have to battle a wind-blown mass of soaking wet plastic that threatens to become airborne at any moment!

3. A second ground cloth is additional weight and bulk you don't need on a canoe trip.

4. I suggested in the last chapter that holes more often develop from inside packs than from outside. The same is true of tent floors! The extra thickness provided by a four-mil-thick, interior plastic ground cloth will prevent thorns and pine cones from puncturing the nylon tent floor.

Add Extra Stake Loops and Guy Points to Your Tent

Sew nylon "storm loops" to critical places like the center sidewall and hem. The more stake points you have along the perimeter, the tighter your tent will stay in a storm. Most tents have only three or four stakes per side; five is better!

Wherever possible, attach storm lines to the *metal framework* of the tent, not the rainfly. It's an advantage if you can Velcro storm loops to adjacent poles, as illustrated in **Figure 10-1**. This transfers wind stress from the nylon fly to the metal frame. A stock Eureka Timberline tent, pitched on an exposed site and rigged with the customary eight stakes and no guylines, will often bend poles and become airborne when winds reach 25 miles per hour. Add the extra stakes and storm lines, suggested in Figure 10-1, and it may stand firm in winds of twice that speed!

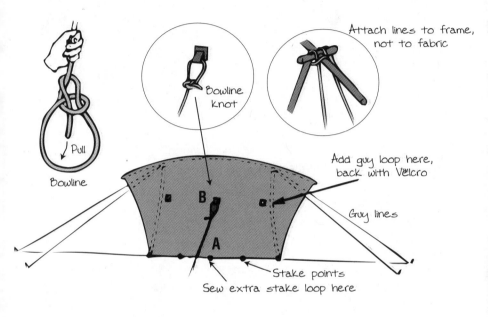

Figure 10-1. Stormproofing the Eureka Timberline.

Double Stake Your Tent on Soft Ground

Two stakes per loop—each through a separate hole, and at a different angle—double the surface area and holding power in soft ground. On rock or sand, try the method illustrated in **Figure 10-2**. If you tie 3-foot lengths of parachute cord to each stake loop, *before* your canoe trip, you won't have to mess with cutting and tying these anchor lines in a rain storm!

Don't Leave Home Without Rain Tarps!

One or two "customized" nylon tarps, with enough cord and stakes to rig them, will provide a dry place to cook and get out of the weather. The alternative to a tarp is to doghouse it in your tent until the storm subsides.

Here are a couple of tricks for rigging tarps:

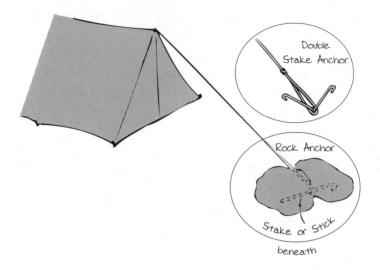

Figure 10-2. Soft ground tent anchors.

1. The corner grommets of your tarp won't tear loose in high winds if you tie the leading edge of the tarp to a tight rope, as illustrated in **Figure 10-3**.

2. If you carry two tarps, overlap them (about a foot) at the ridge and rig them lean-to style, as illustrated in **Figure 10-4**. Two 10 x 12 foot tarps will comfortably accommodate nine people if pitched in this manner. Or, if you have the luxury of an open spot where you can pitch tarps near the campfire, try this: pitch one tarp lean-to style, facing the fire. "Float" the second tarp overhead to provide a horizontal awning. If you leave a generous air space between the overlapped portions of the two tarps, smoke from a rock-backed campfire will be drawn out through the hole rather than into the shelter. My book *Camping's Top Secrets* details this procedure.

Campfires

A Hand Axe and Folding Saw Will Simplify Making Fire in the Rain

If you're tripping in the heart of Canada where dead, downed wood is everywhere, you can probably eliminate the axe. But it's a blessing if you camp

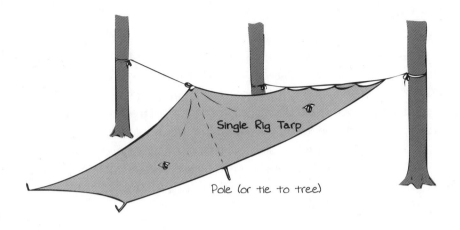

Single Rig Tarp

Pole (or tie to tree)

Figure 10-3.

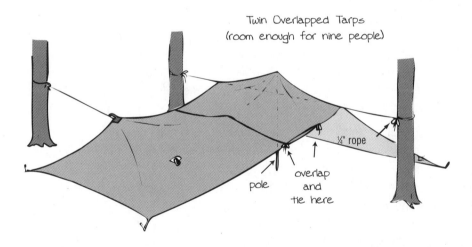

Twin Overlapped Tarps
(room enough for nine people)

¼" rope

pole

overlap
and
tie here

Figure 10-4.

on heavily used sites in the Boundary Waters where all the good wood has been picked over, and making fire means splitting logs to get at the dry heartwood inside.

Admittedly, an axe in the hands of a fool is dangerous to flesh and vegetation—good reasons why federal authorities want to outlaw all choppers. Nonetheless, thousands of experienced campers use axes responsibly. I've always carried a hand axe on my canoe trips and have never had an "axident"—good fortune that I attribute to a rigid policy that does not allow chopping.

First, Locate Dry Wood!

In the days before environmental concerns, birch bark torn from trees, wilted cedar foliage, and dry pine needles scraped from the forest floor were all acceptable fire-making materials. So were dead twigs gathered from the base of conifer trees and wood robbed from beavers' dams. Taking these materials is not an acceptable practice in the BWCA. Indeed, any activity that degrades the look of the land is ecologically unacceptable, and may even be illegal.

To find "good" firewood, locate a *dead, downed tree*, out of sight of tents and trails, and saw off the longest limb you can carry. Avoid wood that touches the ground as it is apt to be rotten.

Please don't be tempted by downed wood along the lakeshore or at the edge of your campsite. Your fresh cuttings will take the wildness out of the wilderness for all who follow!

Use this method to cut and split your firewood.

1. Saw the dead wood branch or bole into foot-long sections. Stand a piece on end, preferably on a heavy, split log base.

2. Gently bury the tip of the axe blade in the end grain and firmly grasp the handle with both hands. Now, ask your friend to pound the blade on through with a small log.

To split fine kindling safely, set the wood to be split upright on a log and hold it in place with a long stick. Then, come down lightly with the hatchet. If you miss your target, you won't cut yourself!

Splitting wood to get at the dry heartwood is the most practical way to make and maintain a campfire in severe weather. Large axes are dangerous and unnecessary. Any tool that's used for "chopping" can slip. And cut! When used as prescribed, the maligned little hand axe is a safe and efficient splitting tool.

If You Want a Really Great Axe!

Gransfors Bruk of Sweden makes the best axes on the planet. My Gransfors Wildlife Hatchet has a 14-inch select hickory handle and a one-pound hand-forged blade that is hardened to R57C, which is harder than conventional axes and as hard as most good knives! The hatchet came from the factory shaving sharp—no kidding. It literally blows small logs apart! And its fine, keen blade will slice a tomato better than most hunting knives I've used. This superbly balanced hatchet is quite remarkable. A hand-riveted, full grain leather sheath protects both the blade and you!

Gransfors makes many different sizes and styles of axes, including special models for skinning large game and serious wood splitting. The spectacular Gransfors Splitting Axe is the supreme tool for those who heat their homes with wood—it's superior to any maul you can buy. See Appendix 2 for Gransfors's address.

Fire-Making Tips

1. The trunk of the balsam fir tree has resin blisters that contain highly flammable pitch. Lance a blister with a sharp stick, collect the resin, and use it to start your fire. Sap weepings attract insects, so please reserve this procedure for genuine emergencies!

2. Search the woods for a dead conifer stump. Roots concentrate resin (pitch), which burns violently. A few sticks of "pitch wood" will ignite wet wood and fuel a campfire for hours.

3. Cedar is the firewood of choice in the Boundary Waters. It contains volatile resins that burn violently, even when the wood is damp. Cedar cuts and splits more easily than other woods and it doesn't produce sparks that can set the woods on fire. Learn to identify this wonderful, straight-grained wood with the fibrous bark.
   It won't take you long to discover that green cedar boughs burn vigorously, even when soaking wet. However, picking green foliage is unethical, illegal (there is a costly fine), and it damages the trees! As mentioned, you can easily obtain dry kindling from dead wood splittings. Fine shavings, whittled from cedar heartwood, may be the best tinder of all.

4. Carry a butane lighter, a tube of Mautz Fire Ribbon (a chemical fire starter), and a large plumber's candle, and you'll have no trouble making fire in any weather!

Bothersome Beasts and Ornery Stingers!

Bothersome Beasts

Quick! What do you think people fear most about camping in the Boundary Waters? If you said "bears," you're probably right! Some people are afraid they'll be eaten alive by them, others are worried that bruins will devour their food. The truth is, most bears are afraid of people and so keep pretty well hidden, at least during the day. It's at night, when you're asleep, that they become bold enough to raid your camp.

In my experience, the outfitter- and government-recommended rigamarole of caching food packs in trees, or on a pole or line strung between trees, is a waste of time and energy. Bears—and other bothersome beasts—won't get your food if you follow a few simple rules.

1. Keep a clean camp. Pack out or burn all leftover food. If this is impractical, bury food wastes at least 150 feet from camp and water. And never throw leftover food down Forest Service box latrines. As mentioned in Chapter 5, bears will knock over toilet boxes and climb into the pits to get edibles. The result is an indescribable mess!

2. Don't leave food in your tent! Even toothpaste and gum may attract hungry animals. Bears will tear your tent apart to get food!

3. Some canoeists place food packs under an overturned canoe and set cooking pots on the craft to function as a "night alarm" system. The idea is that if a bear comes along, it will be scared off by the sound of falling metal. Don't you believe it! Camp bears are not afraid of loud noises. If a bear can't figure out how to get food from under your canoe, it may pounce on or bite at the craft. A powerful black bear can probably chew through a Royalex or fiberglass canoe!

4. Animals learn from past experience where campers put their food. Once they discover some scraps, they'll be back for more. Ever notice how

birds, mice, and squirrels hang around the picnic table when people are present? Moving the table a few yards won't help, but eating in a place that is unfamiliar to animals will!

Fortunately, you can outsmart bothersome beasts by simply putting *odor-free* food in an unfamiliar place. For example, bears know from past experience that many campers put their food in trees. *Certain* trees! On popular campsites there is often only one tree with limbs high enough to discourage a determined bruin, and every canoe party hangs their food packs from it.

"Soon as it gets dark, I'll climb up there and get those packs," thinks the bear. And later, she—or one of her cubs—usually does. Black bears are good climbers and they're very skilled at getting food packs out of trees! Bears learn to identify the rope that holds the food pack. They use their claws or teeth to sever the rope and send the pack crashing down. Suzanne Charle, writing in *The New York Times,* reported that bears in Yosemite "have elaborate schemes for getting food.... One time-honored precaution, hanging bags of food from a rope high in a tree, is now seen as useless. Local residents call the food bags 'bear piñatas.' The bears chew off the rope that has been attached elsewhere, or chew off the branch that is supporting the bag.... If the limbs are small, they'll send the cubs out. If that doesn't work, they'll just climb above the bags, launch themselves out of the tree and grab the bags on the way down."

Backpacker Magazine reports, "Bears in the High Peaks region of New York's Adirondack Mountains . . . have learned to associate white bear-bagging rope with free delivery of a tasty treat; one swipe and a meal drops from the sky. Clever backpackers are now stringing two lines: a white one to fake out the bears, and a black rope to hang food in a separate tree."

As I said, bears are very adept at getting food packs out of trees!

To outfox an experienced camp bear, simply break familiar memory patterns: *Don't put your food in the same place as everyone else*!

One solution is to take food packs out of the camp area, well away from hiking trails, game paths, and human traffic. Be sure to seal your food in plastic so there are no odors. The Forest Service wants you to hang your food packs at least twelve feet off the ground, five feet below a branch, and ten feet from the nearest tree trunk. Finding a tree that meets these specifications is like searching for the ideal campsite—a breezy, sun-exposed level spot with good drainage, convenient access to water, and enough tree cover to discourage high winds.

A perfect "bear tree" is as elusive as the perfect campsite! Simply lofting your pack into a convenient limb or, up to a pole or tight rope strung between two trees, will not deter a determined bear if everyone else uses the same system! On the other hand, grounding food packs where bears don't expect to find them works like magic.

From 1973 to 1987, friend Al Todnem and I each took two seven-day canoe trips with teenagers into the BWCA. That's four weeks per summer—fifty-six weeks for the two of us. To this, add eleven weeks of canoe trips made solo or with friends. The total was sixty-seven weeks, or 1.3 years in the BWCA.

Bear problems? Absolutely none. Zero.

My method is to break the classical conditioning habit by grounding food packs in an unexpected place. This discourages bears, mice, raccoons, birds, and other critters. Indeed, I can happily report that in forty-one years of canoeing, I have never lost *anything* to wild animals. And this includes close encounters with two BWCA black bears, one Saskatchewan black bear, four tundra grizzlies in the Northwest Territories, seven Hudson Bay–area polar bears, and a small pack of wolves near James Bay, Ontario. These are the bear facts!

If you're still intent on treeing your food packs, just remember not to use the same tree as everyone else! Frankly, I'll stand by my statistics and suggest that lofting food into a tree each night is a good way to consume precious time that you could use swimming, drinking coffee, or staring deep into a flickering fire.

Certainly, no method of caching food is foolproof. Some campers will set their food packs right by a mainstream animal trail, thinking they've put them out of harm's way. Every system requires common sense, and some campers have none. Animals are creatures of habit—they return to where they are regularly fed. If you put food where they expect it, don't be surprised if they get it!

If simply taking your food out of camp and hiding it works so well, then why doesn't the Forest Service recommend this method? It's simple, really: The feds are concerned about *your* safety, not the safety of your food. A policy that keeps campers in tents and food packs in distant trees eliminates most bear encounters.

My friend Tom Anderson, Director of the Rose and Lee Warner Nature Center in Marine, Minnesota, has written a wonderful book entitled *Black Bears: Seasons in the Wild*, which I commend to your attention. I've camped with Tom on many occasions, most recently on a canoe trip through polar bear country near Hudson Bay. Tom never once suggested that we tree our packs, though he recommends it in his book. When I asked him why, he quietly told me it was "expected," then made me promise never to tell a soul. Sorry, Tom, too bad I didn't sign a blood oath!

How To Tell if a Bear Might Visit Your Campsite

It's a good idea to check out a prospective campsite before you commit to it for the night. Look for paper, plastic, foil, and food remains in and around the fire grate, picnic table, and box latrine. Be sure to scrutinize the toilet pit for food wastes. There should be none! Check the shallow water along shore for fish viscera and food. If you see significant foreign matter, move on to cleaner grounds. On the other hand, if everything is in good order, and you follow suit with a clean, odorless camp, it's almost certain you *won't* see a bear!

What To Do if a Bear Comes into Camp

Odds are the bear will come while you're asleep, possibly with a cub or two in tow. If you sense the presence of a bear, stay calm. It's your food that the bear wants, not you! My somewhat casual procedure goes something like this:

I throw on some clothes, grab a flashlight, and noisily emerge from my tent, curious to see the show. My dried food is vacuum-sealed in plastic and secured in plastic-lined Duluth packs that are scattered on the ground, outside my camp-site. There are no food odors or visible food containers (packs!) to attract a hungry bruin, so there's little cause for concern. Invariably, the intruder will search the usual places—the "bear pole" or "tree," picnic table, fireplace, and box latrine—then, finding nothing, leave with a discouraged grunt. This scenario almost always plays true. It is possible that a bear might get mad, so I keep my distance. I make the bear aware of my presence but I do not intimidate it by throwing rocks or shining a light into its eyes. I just watch and wait. In ten minutes or so, the show will be over, the bear will leave, and I will return to bed.

Maybe one bear in 10,000 actively seeks human prey. It happened in the Boundary Waters in 1987 and in Algonquin Provincial Park in 1992. The BWCA attack was unusual because a father and son watched the bear (a small female) peer at them from the edge of the forest for several minutes before she attacked. Convinced that the bear was merely curious, the man sent his son to gather firewood. As soon as the boy was out of sight, the bear galloped in. The man leaped into the lake and the bear followed. The son rushed back, beating the bear with a canoe paddle and getting his dad into a canoe. That fast action saved the man's life. When Forest Service personnel later killed the bear, they discovered she was starving.

A more tragic episode occurred in Algonquin Provincial Park in 1992. A young man and woman were killed and eaten by a black bear while they were setting up camp. The two campers were experienced and they had a clean camp. The bear was a healthy animal of average size and weight. Why the unprovoked attack? We can only surmise that there are crazy bears like there are crazy people. Fortunately, there aren't very many of them.

These grisly cases make news precisely because they are so rare. You are more likely to drown, be struck by lightning, or killed by a falling tree than attacked by a black bear. Nonetheless, if you are attacked, the rule is to *fight with all your might*! Do not lie down and play dead!

Black bears often "mock" charge: They woof loudly and menacingly clack their teeth as they gallop toward you. The formula solution is to stand your ground, spread your arms wide, and confidently call, "Whoa, bear!" Above all, *don't run*! Doing so may well provoke an attack.

Some Final "Protective" Thoughts

1. Bears don't like large numbers of people. Two people are more likely to be attacked than six. If a bear comes into your camp, huddle together and spread your arms wide, so as to make a large presence. *Do not* throw rocks at the bear, as advised in the Boundary Waters Canoe Area training film, *Leave No Trace—A Wilderness Ethic*. I did this once, years ago, and the bear nearly had me for dinner!

2. You are safer sleeping inside a tent than on open ground, especially in grizzly country. Evidently, the big bears mistake a human in a sleeping bag for their natural food.

3. Women who are menstruating may be at greater risk from bear attacks, though there is no clear evidence to support this. Stephen Herrero addresses this topic in detail in his highly acclaimed book, *Bear Attacks*.

4. Pepper spray (sometimes called "bear mace"), contains about one percent capsaicin—the flaming-hot ingredient in red pepper. It is very effective if properly used. Herrero observed that even a dangerous mother with cubs will run away from the spray more than 80 percent of the time. Herrero did not find a single case where spraying a bear with pepper enraged it and made it more aggressive.

The large, 230-gram (net weight) can sprays up to 30 feet; smaller pocket sized models go half as far and deliver less pepper. Get the largest can you can find! Do not test-fire a can of pepper spray near your camp or keep a test-fired can in your tent. Recent studies suggest that while bears don't like to be sprayed with pepper, they do like the taste of it. Evidently, bears like spicy food too! When rafters in Alaska sprayed their rafts with pepper to keep bears away, the bears devoured the rafts! Bears also destroyed an outhouse that was sprayed with pepper.

If you're going to Quetico, be aware that pepper spray is illegal in Canada but "animal protection devices" are not! Canadian officials will allow cayenne-based products if they are clearly labeled "For Use on Animals" and have a pest control number printed on the label. Not all U.S. pepper sprays meet Canadian requirements, and some that do meet the requirements don't have pest control numbers. Check with the manufacturer of the product if you have any doubts.

"Bear mace" is available at many outdoor stores and western U.S. national park shops. I rely on a 230-gram can of Counter Assault (there's a bear on the label!). See Appendix 2 for sources.

One last tip. It may seem too obvious, but don't trigger the pepper spray if the wind is blowing in your face!

Ornery Stingers

There's a T-shirt you may see in Minnesota that bears a chest-filling likeness of a female mosquito and the legend *Minnesota State Bird*. It's no joke. The usual precautions—cover bare skin, slather on gobs of repellent, don't go out alone after dark and stay clear of swampy areas—do reduce encounters with these giant beasts. But the truth is, canoes and insects go hand in hand. It's a cruelty nature bestows upon Boundary Waters paddlers in return for the good times she provides.

Fortunately, bugs nearly always disappear when the sun comes out and the wind blows up. Build a smoldering fire and the usually determined critters chicken out and zoom to parts unknown. Retire to your screened-in tent and you can rest in peace until nature calls.

Frankly, an oblivious attitude is your best defense. Think "bugs don't bother me, bugs don't bother me!" and you won't notice if they do. But mix bad psychology with an ornery disposition, and the pesky critters will devour your hide!

Beyond attitude, there is science, and the usual array of protective measures. Topping the list is a *compact* head net. Bulky, military styles with draw cord hems that button down to breast pockets are a nuisance in the Boundary

Waters where head nets go on and off with each passing wave of insect fighter planes. A simple rectangular net that can quickly be wadded to fist size and stuffed into a hat crown or shirt pocket is best.

Tightly woven cotton-polyester or nylon clothing will keep most bugs at bay. Clothes don't get much more bug-proof than inexpensive GI fatigues and chinos. Some bite-sensitive paddlers subscribe to overkill and seal pant hems and shirt sleeves with Velcro strips. But few days are buggy enough to warrant this practice. If bugs drive you batty, you may want to get a netted "bug shirt," which you can wear while you paddle. The Original Bug Shirt (see Appendix 2), which is made from mosquito netting and ultralight, bleached white cotton, is one of the best. It features a zippered hood with integral face net. Closures at the wrist and waist provide an impenetrable seal.

The color of your clothes is important. Generally, dark hues attract insects. Tans, grays, greens, and powder blues neither attract not repel, but darker shades of blue, black, or deep red drive bugs wild. Navy blue—the most popular of all outdoor colors—is absolutely the worst color of all!

After clothing, your next line of defense is a good insect repellent. Those high in the active ingredient DEET (n,n diethyl-m-toluamide) work best, though there are some health concerns. DEET can irritate sensitive skin, and high concentrations of the chemical produce allergic reactions in some people. Very young children and sensitive adults should use citronella-based formulas. In addition, DEET can dissolve certain kinds of plastics and paints.

In my travels to the Northwest Territories of Canada, I've field-tested just about every insect repellent known to man. Here's a summary of my findings, which I gathered from bites on my own body!

1. Pure or nearly pure DEET repels bugs best, but it is so caustic to skin, plastic pocketknife handles, the plastic frames of glasses, synthetic long underwear, and plastic canoe parts, that I refuse to use it. Mild, cream-based repellents with 25 to 50 percent DEET work nearly as well as full strength and they last much longer. They are also much less expensive than high-DEET products.

2. I dislike the oily feel of repellents, so I usually just daub the chemicals on my clothing—shirt cuffs, pant leg hems, inside my hat brim, and a large red handkerchief that I wear around my neck. This keeps most insects away from my face, wrists, and ankles.

3. Aerosol spray cans, though technically legal in the Boundary Waters, are not worth bringing along. Read the label and you'll see how ineffective and pricey they are. And, there's a bulky can to pack out!

Black Flies and No-See-Ums

Black flies are more at home on fast-moving rivers than lakes, so they seldom occur in epidemic proportions in the Boundary Waters. However, when these pesky gnats do appear, head nets or "bug jackets" (the kind anglers wear) are your only salvation. Repellents, by and large, merely discourage black flies. I've seen these ugly little insects swim in 50 percent DEET, then get up and fly away!

Black flies have an unusual habit of flying or climbing to the highest place. They'll swarm around your head. Raise up your hat on a canoe paddle and they'll follow it. If you're very clever, you may be able to use this tactic to shag them on to a nearby friend!

If black flies get into your tent, don't panic. After a few minutes, they'll settle on the bug screen and begin to climb skywards. Let them have their little walk. When they reach the top of the net, slowly unzip the screen and heartlessly toss them back into the cruel world. You're ahead of the game if your tent has two entrances. If the tent fills with bugs, open both entrances and leave the tent for a few minutes. The bugs will fly through your tent and exit through the downwind door. When the bugs are gone, close the upwind door from outside the tent. Then close the downwind door. You'll enjoy a relatively bug-free environment if you always use the downwind door when you enter and exit your tent.

When Repellents Fail, Retire to Your "Susie Bug Net"!

First, you apply repellents to exposed skin. As more insects home in, you add a head net, then a DEET-impregnated bug jacket. Ultimately, you rant and swear, and in disgust retire to your no-see-um–proof tent. Meanwhile, friends nearby enjoy a bug-free after-dinner brandy and a glorious sunset inside their "Susie bug net" (**Figure 11-1**)—personal bug armor designed by my wife, Sue Harings.

To make a Susie bug net you'll need a piece of mosquito netting 7 feet wide and 10 feet long, plus enough ⅛-inch-diameter shock cord to span the hem. Don't use no-see-um net; it's not strong enough and you can't see through it. Fold the netting lengthwise to produce a rectangular sheet that measures about 5 feet wide by 7 feet long. Sew up two adjacent sides, hem the bottom, and install the bungee cord in the hem. The finished net will weigh less than a pound and compress to football size.

Here are some uses for your Susie bug net:

1. Eat inside it; there's room for two adults or a pack of kids.

2. Sleep out under the stars. The net covers you from head to toe. Cinch the bungee cord tightly around the boot of your sleeping bag.

3. Use it as a "porta potty" when bugs are bad. It fully encompasses the official Forest Service "throne."

4. Swim in it! Amble to the beach as a ghostly apparition in your Susie bug net. Wear your life vest and you'll float confidently inside your bug armor. When you've had your swim, step assertively ashore and drape the netting over a rock to dry.

5. Gently lay the net over breads, cheese, and lunch meats to keep flies away.

Figure 11-1. The Susie Bug Net.

6. Rig a tripod inside and you have a tiny, bug-proof tipi in which to wash dishes, cook, and make equipment repairs.

Protective netting is essential if there are children or bug-sensitive adults in your party. With a little practice you can hike, run, and even paddle a canoe while wearing a Susie bug net! Roll and stuff your Susie bug net under a pack flap so it will be available at meals and rest stops.

No-See-Ums

No-see-ums are similar to black flies, but they are much smaller and less menacing. Whereas black fly bites may bleed and swell for days, no-see-um bites sting for a few seconds and produce short-lived red welts. But at their worst, no-see-ums attack by the thousands and they're so small they fly right through standard mesh tent screens, head nets, and even Susie bug nets!

The solution is to cover up completely *and* apply repellents on exposed skin and wide-mesh mosquito screens. Most modern tents have fine-mesh netting that discourages no-see-ums and the free passage of air. Unfortunately, no-see-ums usually appear on hot, muggy days when you'd give anything for a welcome breeze. So in the end, it's a toss-up: If your tent is equipped with fine mesh netting, you get no no-see-ums and no ventilation. If it has standard mosquito netting, you enjoy a cool night of swatting bugs!

Frankly, no-see-ums are relatively rare in the Boundary Waters. When they do appear, you can usually discourage them by treating standard mesh mosquito screens with repellents. Or simply close the nylon door panel, which, of course, stifles the air.

Dangers, Safety, and First Aid

Newcomers to the Boundary Waters commonly express three fears: bugs, bears, and bad weather. Bugs and bears, as we've learned from the last chapter, are less a real threat than a perceived one. The *real* dangers are lightning storms and whitecaps, capsizing far from shore in frigid water, high winds, falling trees ("widow-makers"), hypothermia-producing cold, wrecking your canoe in a rapid, and being injured while portaging or swimming. There are also burns, cuts, waterborne parasites, eye injuries, and, God forbid, a gasoline stove that explodes in your face (it happened to me!). Any one of these events may end your canoe trip on the spot and leave you wondering how you'll get back to your car. Here's how to avoid these common dangers—and to treat their effects when you can't!

Swimming Don'ts!

1. *Absolutely no diving—ever!* I once reprimanded some teenagers for diving off a high cliff on Gunflint Lake. Their leader curtly advised me to "stay out of our business," so I shut my mouth and paddled on to my campsite, which was about half a mile away. Later that evening, two canoes full of kids from the group I earlier admonished stopped at my camp and tearfully asked directions to the public landing. They told me that shortly after I left, one of the boys dove headfirst into a submerged rock. The adult leader flagged down the driver of a passing fishing boat who took him and the boy to the road head and on to the hospital in Grand Marais. The leader told the kids to paddle out and wait for him at nearby Gunflint Lodge.

After our trip we were horrified to learn that the boy died from the concussion. This solitary event suggests that diving of any kind is unsafe on a canoe trip!

2. *Don't swim barefooted!* On the first day of my first school-sponsored canoe trip, a fourteen-year-old girl badly cut her big toe while swimming barefoot in a rocky area. Since then, I have required that shoes be worn while swimming. I suggest you adopt a similar policy.

3. *Don't swim alone!* This rule is cardinal in every tripping camp in the country, and for good reason. If suddenly you cramp while swimming, or a breeze blows you far from shore, you'll wish you had a friend to tow you in or yell a warning. If you want to cover all bases, wear your life jacket when you swim.

4. *Don't go into the water until you have identified a safe escape route to shore.* I've watched tired swimmers struggle to obtain a secure foothold on sharp or slippery rocks—another reason to wear shoes when you swim! I sometimes tie a long "exit rope" to a heavy rock or tree to help swimmers climb ashore.

Lightning

Any canoe on open water is a perfect lightning rod, so get ashore at the first hint of thunder. Nonetheless, converting advice to practice isn't easy if there are big waves and a rocky shoreline. You often have no choice but to paddle on to a campsite, portage, or protected cove.

A "cone of protection" extends from the tops of the tallest trees or hills outward about forty-five degrees in all directions (**Figure 12-1**). Paddle within this protected zone, but not so close to its center that lightning may jump to you. Lightning can jump 30 feet or more, so 50 to 100 feet from shore may be the best place to be. When you find a place to land, seek a low-lying spot away from the tall trees near the water's edge. A rocky overhang provides good protection and makes a fine umbrella under which to wait out the rain.

If You Awaken to a Lightning Storm

Say you're awakened from a sound sleep by the loud crack of thunder. Rain is coming down in sheets and white lightning dances across the sky. What to do?

The textbook solution is to leave your tent and wait out the storm in a low, protected area. But your tightly pitched tent is dry inside and standing firm in the persistent wind. Wearily, you unzip a window and peer at the worsening storm.

"S'pose we should get outa here before we get fried?" you remark to your friend, who has just begun to stir.

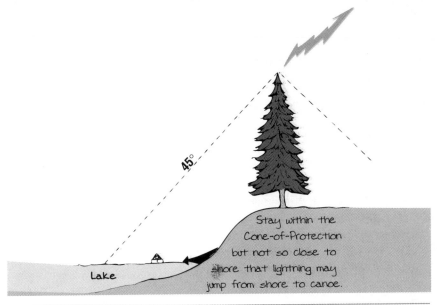

Stay within the Cone-of-Protection but not so close to shore that lightning may jump from shore to canoe.

Lake

Figure 12-1. When lightning strikes.

"You gotta be kidding," comes the sleepy answer. "Leave this tent? Never! See ya in the morning, buddy."

If you plan to stay put, take these precautions: Sit up on your *dry* foam sleeping pad. Draw up your knees so that only your buttocks and soles of your feet touch the insulated pad. If you do get burned from a nearby strike, the electricity will miss your heart. Be aware that this precaution won't work if your bedding gets wet—a condition you can prevent by always using a plastic ground cloth *inside* your tent!

First Aid for Lightning Burns

Lightning hits a tree 30 feet from a tent located at the opposite end of your campsite. You dress hastily and run to your friends, one of whom is unresponsive and not breathing. One of his shoes is missing and there is a small, deep burn on the sole of his foot.

Diagnosis? Electrocution—and cardiac arrest!

High-voltage electricity usually kills people by producing cardiac arrest. It may also paralyze the respiratory system. If the person is alive, the burns are probably minor and can be attended to later. Your immediate concern is to get the person's heart and respiratory system functioning. *Begin CPR immediately!* If you can restore heart rhythm and breathing, you can probably save your friend.

This accomplished, keep the patient warm and send for help immediately. Electrocution may cause disorientation, coma, seizures, and spinal cord injuries. It may also rupture the eardrums. All you can do until help arrives is to keep your friend immobilized and warm, and convince him that he'll be okay.

Widow-Makers

Widow-maker is forestry slang for a wind-downed tree that gets caught in the branches of another as it falls. The first good breeze drops some widow-makers, others remain hung up for decades. Occasionally, you'll find these dangerous snags poised menacingly over beautiful tent sites. I caution you to resist the urge to cut down or remove branches from these trees, or to pitch your camp in the probable path of their fall. Widow-makers are under tremendous tension. If one splits under the pressure of a saw, or comes crashing down on you at night, you may awaken in another world! Snag removal is a job for Forest Service professionals!

When Your Canoe Becomes a Kite!

I was napping on Miles Island on Saganaga Lake on a testy June day when a sudden squall came up. I always make it a practice to tie my overturned, beached canoe to a tree before I wander off or retire to my tent. But this time I didn't follow my own advice.

Suddenly, the wind lashed out with uncommon fury and turned my 18-foot lightweight aluminum canoe into a kite! The craft sailed overhead, end for end, then dropped into the waves about 100 feet from shore. Barefoot and clad in a swimsuit, I quickly zipped on my life vest and dove in after it. Thank goodness there was a long tracking line with which to tow the canoe ashore. I suffered a bruised foot and badly injured pride. I also learned to practice what I preach!

Inverting and tying unattended canoes to a tree or boulder is an expedition axiom that every canoeist should embrace. Every season in the BWCA, canoes blow out to sea. And red-faced canoeists swim after them!

On a similar note, never store your paddles in the open or on a sloping rock where wind or rain could carry them into the lake. Lay your paddles on the ground next to your tent. If you have bent-shaft paddles, turn them *blade-up* so they won't break if you accidentally step on them.

Safety with Edged Tools

Whittling

Cuts from whittling are the most common injury among teenagers in the BWCA. The rule of thumb is to bring *three* Band-Aids per kid. Or carry fewer bandages and outlaw whittling!

for safety sake

Figure 12-2

Don't Lose Your Knife

You won't lose your pocketknife if you tie it to a nylon lanyard attached to your belt. Or, place the knife in your pocket and stuff a large handkerchief on top.

Axe Safety

If you use your hand axe as a simple splitting wedge, as suggested in Chapter 10, you'll eliminate most accidents. Keep your axe sheathed and in a pack when it's not being used. *Never* leave an axe stuck in a log—someone could trip over it! If you must set down an unsheathed axe for a short time, place the axe on its side, blade tucked under a heavy log or rock, as illustrated in **Figure 12-2.**

A Safe Place for Your Folding Saw

Most canoeists leave their folding saw by the woodpile, figuring it will come in handy later—a practice that can be dangerous, especially if there are exposed teeth and failing light. A colleague learned this lesson on a canoe trip with teenagers. Two kids were horsing around when one lost his balance and fell, lightly brushing the saw, which was leaning, teeth out, against a tree. Fortunately the youngster only suffered a minor cut. Figure 12-3 suggests two reasonably safe ways to store a saw when it is not folded and packed!

Water Quality

More than 200,000 people a year use the Boundary Waters—reason enough to boil, filter, or chemically treat every drop of water you drink. Water tests conducted in the early 1980s by my own ninth-grade environmental science students suggest that water taken from shallow lakes, beaver streams, and near popular campsites is not safe to drink. Play the odds long enough and

Figure 12-3. Saw safety.

you'll probably get burned.

Nonetheless, a lot of canoeists draw water where they find it and don't give quality a second thought. A minority (myself included) boil or filter questionable water and follow these rules religiously:

1. Never take water from shallows or within 100 feet of a campsite. Sometimes, I weight my water pail with a rock and submerge the pail thirty feet or more on a long rope.

2. Don't drink "green" water. It contains algae that harbor microorganisms. Water colored brown from natural tree-produced tannins is fine.

3. Friendly microorganisms need oxygen to decompose wastes in water. For this reason, water taken from wavy or turbulent places is more likely to be safe than that drawn from stagnant areas or wind-protected bays.

4. Don't take water from beaver streams! Beaver are the favored host of

Giardia lamblia—a protozoan that can make you plenty sick.

5. Ultraviolet light kills microorganisms. Take your drinking water from a sunny place!

Water Treatment Procedures

Boiling: Bring the water to a minimal boil and you'll kill everything except the most resistant spores. Fortunately, these are almost never present in the wilderness—they can only be destroyed by pressurized heat above the boiling point. If you need more heat than 212 degrees F, you need a pressure cooker!

Chemicals: All chemicals make water taste bad—reason enough to avoid them. Boiling and germicidal filters are faster and more reliable, and they preserve the good fresh taste you drove hundreds of miles to experience!

Filters: Most filtration units are cumbersome, delicate, slow to use, and hard to clean. There are exceptions, notably the high-speed PUR "Explorer," which filters one liter of water per minute and cleans in seconds with a twist of the pump handle. The PUR "Scout" and "Hiker," which are smaller, less expensive versions of the "Explorer," are also excellent.

PUR filters received worldwide attention in 1989 when two shipwrecked sailors relied on its manually operated desalination pump to survive 66 days in a life raft adrift in the Pacific Ocean. The PUR combines microfiltration with an antimicrobial tri-iodine resin system that kills bacteria and infectious viruses. A replaceable carbon filter absorbs the objectionable iodine aftertaste.

Medicine for the Boundary Waters

Wilderness first-aid classes tend to emphasize bone-crushing falls and internal injuries, which are more often associated with hiking and mountaineering accidents than with the common mishaps of the Boundary Waters.

For example, in twenty years of guiding canoe trips, no one in my charge has ever suffered a broken limb, head injury, or pulmonary disorder. But I have treated scores of blisters, sprains, scratched corneas, ear infections (swimmer's ear), insect bites, burns, embedded fishhooks, and illness due to waterborne parasites. These are the medical problems that everyone who treks to the Boundary Waters should be prepared to treat.

In preparing this section, I kept uppermost in mind that:

1. Most outdoors people have little in-depth knowledge of first aid and no inclination to learn. It follows that wilderness first-aid procedures should be easy to master, quick to administer, and correct!

2. Sanitary conditions are difficult to attain in the woods. Nonetheless, many first-aid techniques require sterile technique. Canoeists need to know simple ways to clean wounds.

3. The wilderness "first aider" must adopt treatment procedures that reflect realistic field conditions. For example, you may not be able to leave a taped-down fishhook embedded in the skin or keep a victim off a bad sprain if he or she must help paddle and portage the canoe and do camp chores.

4. Most canoeists don't want to carry a sophisticated first-aid kit. If it won't fit in a one-pound coffee can, it will probably be left at home!

Not everyone has the time or discipline to master the advanced medical techniques needed to treat heavy-duty fractures, gashes, and head wounds. However, everyone can, in a few hours, learn how to treat the common ailments that are most likely to be encountered on a canoe trip.

With these thoughts, I offer the following field-proven, physician-recommended techniques for treating the most common backcountry injuries, along with suggestions for building a small but useful first-aid kit. Space does not permit detailing all you need to know about the described conditions. If you're serious about wilderness medicine, you'll seek authoritative knowledge through books. I recommend Dr. William W. Forgey's *Wilderness Medicine: Beyond First Aid*, published by The Globe Pequot Press.

First-Aid Kit: Suggested Contents

An antiseptic, pain reliever, anti-inflammatory drug, and antibiotic ointment, plus an over-the-counter remedy for burns and insect bites, are the major medications you'll need. To this, add an antacid, tape, gauze, compresses, and Band-Aids, and you're set for most emergencies.

The Mini-First-Aid Kit

Here's the bare minimum if you want to go light:

1. 4 eye patches

2. Spenco Second Skin

3. Microfoam tape

4. Triple antibiotic ointment

5. Four Band-Aids

6. Small roll of bandage gauze

7. Aspirin, acetaminophen, or ibuprofen tablets

8. Small tube of Polysporin ophthalmic ointment (Rx), or yellow oxide of mercury—ophthalmic 2 percent (non-Rx)

9. Antacid tablets

First Aid for Common Ailments

Fishhook in the Skin

The common advice is to work the embedded barb through the skin, cut off the barb, and extract the hook. But this won't work if the hook is embedded to the curve. In any case, extraction will be painful unless you irrigate the entrance hole of the fishhook with one to two milliliters of Xylocaine. Wait a few minutes for the drug to take effect, then complete the extraction.

There is, however, a better and virtually painless method of hook extraction that doesn't require Xylocaine. This method is illustrated in **Figure 12-4**.

The procedure is simple:

1. Loop light cord or fish line around the curve of the hook.

2. Push the eye of the hook firmly against the surface of the skin.

3. While holding the shank down, firmly jerk the cord.

This method works so well that the victim often doesn't know when the hook is out!

The "string-pull" technique works best when the hook is stuck in places like the shoulder, back of the head, and parts of the torso and extremities that have little connective tissue. *Don't* use this procedure if the hook is lodged in the fingers or near an eye; in such cases, surgical extraction with Xylocaine is recommended. If you are unsure of your extraction skills, tape the fishhook in place so it won't do further damage and evacuate the victim to a hospital.

Foreign Body in the Eye

First, try to flush out the foreign body with Eye Stream. If that fails, have the

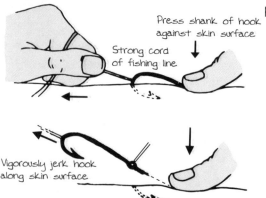

Press shank of hook
against skin surface

Strong cord
of fishing line

Vigorously jerk hook
along skin surface

Figure 12-4. Painless fishhook removal.

patient look straight ahead while you shine a light into the eye from one side. If you see a speck (lift the upper eye lid and check here, too), gently brush it away with a cotton swab. If there is any pain or redness, lace the lower lid with Neosporin ophthalmic ointment (Rx), or yellow oxide of mercury, ophthalmic 2 percent (non-Rx). The patient should close his or her eyes until the medication melts. If pain persists, bandage *both* eyes shut with eye patches and microfoam tape.

Dislocated Shoulder

A dislocated shoulder is one of the most common and painful ailments in canoeing. Relocation is easy if you use the Stimson method illustrated in **Figure 12-5**:

Place the victim face down on a flat, elevated platform. An overturned canoe will do. Tie an approximate ten-pound weight to the wrist of the fully

Figure 12-5. Stimson method to re-locate a dislocated shoulder.

extended arm with a soft neckerchief or padded belt. As the muscles tire, the victim will relax and the shoulder will relocate. What could be simpler? Or safer?

Friction Blister on the Heel

If a friction blister develops, it will have to be lanced. First, wash it with soap and open it along one edge with a sharp penknife. Use your butane lighter to sterilize the knife. Express the fluid then apply triple antibiotic ointment. Top this with a piece of Spenco Second Skin held in place with the Spenco knit bandage.

An alternative method is to clean and lance the blister as above. Apply antibiotic ointment and cover with *two* eye patches and microfoam tape. The combination of patches and tape provides substantial cushioning for the blister site.

Space prohibits detailing all the things you need to know to treat these and other conditions. But I won't omit the best advice of all, which is to *slow down and think before you act.* Avoid the accident and you won't need all that good first-aid gear you brought along!

Signals: When You Need To Bring the Airplane Down!

It was 1967 and my first trip to the Boundary Waters. My friend John Orr and I had just completed the portage into Knife Lake when we came upon a group of teenagers. Amid the canoes and equipment was a stretcher occupied by a fifteen-year-old girl.

The girl told us she had a severe stomach ache and would be okay in a few days. John, an old football coach, questioned her further, then gently touched a side of her abdomen. It was very painful and tender. John's diagnosis was appendicitis.

We suggested that the leaders immediately paddle the girl to Cache Bay Ranger Station, where there was a radio telephone. But, before they could comply, we spotted a Forest Service fire plane overhead. I whipped out my mirror-equipped Silva Ranger compass and flashed the pilot's eye. The plane landed and ferried the youngster to the hospital in Grand Marais. When John and I returned from our trip we learned that the girl's appendix had been removed without complication, and with just hours to spare!

A mirror is well worth bringing along on a Boundary Waters trip. An official military heliograph (the kind with the hole in the center) is much easier to use than a standard mirror. Ultralight signaling mirrors are available at most camping shops.

There are a lot of smoky campfires in the BWCA, so it's doubtful you can bring down a plane or attract a Forest Service canoe with one. However, colored smoke is almost certain to attract help. Orange smoke grenades with fifty-second burning times are available at every marina and sailing shop. You may want to consider carrying some if you will be more than two days from help.

A Magic Day in the BWCA

Sunrise on a quiet lake deep in the heart of the Boundary Waters Canoe Area. Anxious hands, chilled by the day's beginning, slip the trim Kevlar canoe into the champagne-clear water. Only the muffled chirp of a Canada jay testifies to the day's awakening.

You muscle your gear to the water's edge and, with the help of your partner, methodically place it into the canoe. The natural odor of sweat-stained canvas and hand-oiled leather suggests that these old Duluth packs "belong."

It takes less than a minute to orient your map and set a compass bearing to the first portage, which by your calculation is more than two miles away. Briefly, you glance at your watch—it's 7:15 A.M. An hour of casual paddling will bring you to the first carry of the day.

You're paddling stern today, so you have the luxury of a shock-corded thwart that keeps your oriented map from blowing out to sea. Strapped around the thwart is a handy wrist compass that you can read without putting down your paddle.

For a while, you paddle determinedly along, eyes intent on a distant notch on the horizon, beyond which is the portage. Then, suddenly aware that you are hurrying for no reason, you call a pause and laze back in the canoe and drop your arms to your sides, hands immersed wrist-deep in the cool clear water. Every muscle relaxes as your body attunes to the growing warmth of the expanding sun. Overhead, a lone cottony cloud punctuates an ocean of azure. Here, there are no schedules or deadlines to meet, no intellectual discussions or arguments. There is just the magic of the water.

Ultimately, you are awakened by the hushed enthusiasm of your partner. "There, there!" she whispers, pointing to a full-grown moose a hundred feet away. "Freeze—just float," you quietly say. Startled, but unafraid, the huge animal stares curiously your way. Then, with an unhurried air, she swims lazily ashore and disappears into the forest. It is barely 8:00 and already the wind is producing small whitecaps on the formerly placid water. Thank goodness you are now in the lee of the islands. Momentarily, you rest your paddle on the gunnels and study the map. "The portage is in that bay to the right," you call confidently. "No, I think it's over there," answers your partner, who motions toward a narrow stream at left.

Her destination is closer, so you go there first. Sure enough, she is right on target—a small opening near the channel marks the carry.

You put ashore at the 80-rod portage but don't unload the canoe. The rough trail suggests that either few people come this way or there's a "paddle-through" to the next lake. "Let's check out the beaver stream before we carry over," you call enthusiastically.

The stream is clear for the first hundred yards. Then, it disappears in a maze of thick vegetation.

"Think we can get through?" asks your friend.

"Don't know. Wanna try?"

"Sure," comes the ready reply.

At the start, the beaver stream is narrow and deep, with plenty of water to float a canoe. Round the bend, it sprawls to a shallow pond and there's a low dam that you must carry over. Then, you're back in the skinny channel again and it's a smooth ride to the next lake.

Smugly, you congratulate one another on your adventurous spirits and the portage you didn't make!

It is noon and the high golden sun has flooded the day with warmth and light. High in the crown of a lofty white pine is a huge eagle nest that must weigh a quarter ton. In a flash, a mature bald eagle becomes airborne and silently glides your way. Disturbed by your presence, it emits a concerned "keeow!"

You put ashore on a lichen-splashed outcrop and prepare the lunch. Pita bread laced with vacuum-sealed dill cheese, summer sausage, and spicy brown mustard go down easily with crystal lemonade you mix in a poly bottle. It has been an unusually interesting day so you agree to share one of the six crisp Braeburn apples you have brought along for special occasions.

The meal closes with a thorough policing of the lunch site. Every bit of garbage, from the tiniest twist-tie to the smallest rubber band, is zealously rounded up and placed in a heavy-duty plastic bag to be later burned at the campfire or packed out to civilization. To leave evidence—even the smallest evidence—of humankind on this treasured site is unthinkable. You don't need official rules and preaching to tell you what is right.

By 3:00 in the afternoon you have covered 10 miles, which was your goal for the day. You've run two bouncy rapids, portaged five times, and cheated a sixth carry by paddling the beaver stream to the next lake. High on a proud granite hill, a windward campsite commands a full view of the sparkling lake. "Let's camp there," you say unanimously. Then together you burst out laughing and agree that a long cool swim and coffee brewed fresh over a crackling fire would be a perfect way to end this perfect day. As you put ashore on the idyllic site, you make a pact not to take the day's events too seriously. After all, tomorrow may be another magic day.

# Advice from the Experts

No single book can address everything you need to know to "smooth the way" on a Boundary Waters trip. There are bound to be questions left unanswered. No one has a monopoly on good ideas, so I've asked some very experienced Boundary Waters paddlers for help. The question was, "What advice would you give someone who is about to make his or her first canoe trip into the BWCA?"

Allen Todnem, Hastings, Minnesota

Al Todnem is a high school biology teacher who has guided dozens of school

and church groups on canoe trips into the Boundary Waters. In the early 1980s, Al and I operated a high-adventure canoeing program in Canada for teenagers. Here are Al's tips:

"Preparing meals is easier if you pre-package everything you need for a given meal in one bag. For example, I put one cup of dried breakfast cereal into a resealable bag along with two-thirds cup of powered milk and an appropriate amount of sugar (if needed). I just add one cup of cold or boiling water to make the cereal.

"I pack my extra clothing in strong nylon bags. For example, I have one bag for socks and underwear, another for shirts, and another for trousers and shorts. I keep dirty socks and underwear in a see-through plastic bag. The contents of each bag are labeled. All the small nylon bags go inside one large bag. This method keeps clothing organized and separates dirty items from clean ones.

"It's a good idea to tether a line to your fishing pole and the canoe.

"A small bag of hard candy packed with each breakfast keeps energy flowing smoothly all day long."

Neil Bernstein, Cedar Rapids, Iowa

Neil Bernstein began canoeing the Boundary Waters/Quetico region while working at a girls' camp in northern Wisconsin. During 1974–75, he guided six trips into Quetico Provincial Park that lasted five to fourteen days. Since then, Neil has canoed most of the routes in Quetico. Neil says,

"In 1975, I beached my lightweight Grumman aluminum canoe on a flat, rocky shelf for the night. I turned it over and tied down the bow. A wind kicked up that night, and slammed the canoe around. I ran to the scene as fast as I could, but it was too late—a rock had already beaten a hole in the stern of the canoe! Now, I always pull my canoe well up on shore and tie *both* ends down!"

I asked Neil if he had ever encountered any "life-threatening" situations in the Quetico. He said, "Most problems were the result of people making poor choices—swimming at the base of a rapid where there is a strong current, damaging a canoe while running a rapid, hypothermia, and deep cuts from axes. A fifteen-year-old girl broke an arm while bracing on a log over a portage. Once, I grabbed a canoe full of campers just before it went over a falls. On another occasion, I was confronted by a hungry, aggressive mother bear with cubs during a drought year when natural foods were low."

Ken E. Brown, Dakota, Minnesota

Ken Brown discovered the BWCA in 1993 and he has been going there ever since. His trips usually run for a week and originate off the Arrowhead, Gunflint, and Sawbill trails. Ken commonly travels with a crew of four or six. Ken's tips:

"Take a nylon screen tent, but leave the poles at home. Use trees, rocks, and ingenuity to rig the tent. When entering the screen house, leave the door zipped shut. Just lift the wall and scoot under. It's better to anchor the walls with rocks than to stake them.

"'Gamma Seals' are snap-on lids for five-gallon pails. They make any five-gallon pail watertight and critter-proof. Once secured, they are on to stay. Some sporting goods stores have them. You can use the bucket as a stool in camp or as a small table.

"Bring at least one extra set of car keys, and give them to a friend *before you leave home*. If you lock your keys in your car when you stop for gas, your friend will let you in!

"Carry personal items like toilet paper, lip balm, sunscreen, bug dope, knife, compass, etc. on your person, in a small fanny pack or day pack.

"Bring some paper towels: They are great for cleanup and can be used for toilet paper."

Tom and Sue Chelstrom, Boise, Idaho

Tom and Sue hail from Minnesota where Tom ran the Bloomington R.E.I. store. "Chel," as his friends call him, now manages the new R.E.I. store in Boise, Idaho.

"In the mid 1970s I was doing lots of Boundary Waters trips and fishing was my passion. I was frustrated about how to stow rods securely in the canoe while portaging and still have them instantly accessible for a quick cast. I came up with a simple rod-security device that was a big hit at my Boundary Waters Bound clinics at the Ski Haus in St. Paul in the 1970s, and at R.E.I. in the 1980s. Here's how to make one: Sew a simple nylon sleeve and tie it tightly between  the seats, thwarts, or gunnels. Then slide the rod, with reel and lure attached, into the sleeve. Secure the butt end to your canoe seat with a loop of shock cord tied around the seat.

"When cartopping your canoe, always tie down *both* the bow and stern. Many modern cars have plastic bumpers that won't support "tie-down" bolts or S-hooks. I tie loops of one-inch-wide tubular nylon (climbing) webbing to the uni-body under the hood. Look around and you'll find a bolt or bracket to which you can secure the webbing.

"When cartopping, open the hood, pull out the nylon loops, then close the hood. Run your ropes from the bow of the canoe through these nylon loops.

When not in use, tuck the loops out of sight under the hood. I tie loops to the drain holes on the bottom of the rear bumper to tie the stern down."

Dr. Nick Boismenue and Stephanie Urbonya, Rhinelander, Wisconsin

Steph and Nick have been canoeists all their lives. With their two golden retrievers, they make an annual trip (fly in, paddle out) to Quetico Provincial Park, entering on the north side and paddling out the south side.

"Our water containers are plastic milk jugs—both gallon and half gallon. We stow them in a mesh bag behind the rear seat and just leave them in place when we portage. We take extra caps and extra jugs (a jug will remain watertight for about seven days, then it will begin to leak around the rim). For bowls (eating, mixing, or dog food) we just use other milk jugs with the tops cut off. To store these bowls, just pop them onto the bottom of the full milk jugs. We have found that we can nest up to three bowls together on one milk jug. You can make small bowls from half-gallon jugs and large bowls from gallon jugs. Here's a hint: Don't dip a jug into the water with bowls nested on it—they'll all fall off!

"At our vet's suggestion, we take a high-performance dog food (for sled dogs). This allows us to cut the volume of dog food we need by half. We especially like the foil-packaged, vacuum-sealed, two-pound bags of Pro Plan High Performance Dog Food, which are compact and odorless. We give our dogs cooked instant mashed potatoes, cooked rice, or cooked pasta as extra volume, mixed in with their food every second to third day.

"We carry Granite Gear Kawnipi Packs as chest packs. We slip a small carabiner through one of the plastic D-rings on the webbing straps. We snap our Sierra cups, compass, and other small gear to the carabiner for quick access."

Barry Tungseth, Hastings, Minnesota

Barry has been canoeing the Boundary Waters since the 1960s. He has canoed the Ely, Isabella, Crane Lake, and Gunflint area and has done remote border crossings into Quetico. Barry usually makes two one-week canoe trips each year.

"Go easy with first-timers, especially children. Don't make your trips too ambitious! Practice on a local waterway before you attempt the Boundary Waters. Get your friends used to going without video games, stereo, TV, soda pop, fast food, and the constant noise that accompanies civilization. Some wanna-be Boundary Waters paddlers just can't break with civilization. Better find out now, before you commit them to the remote solitude of the Boundary Waters.

"Let the weakest member of the party set the pace. Don't turn your Boundary Waters experience into a race.

"Look at the positives when making a portage. Don't project a "hurry-up-to-the-other-side" attitude. It's often more fun—and relaxing—to make several trips over a portage with light loads than to power through encumbered with heavy gear. Like good food, small bites taste better!"

Sue Harings, River Falls, Wisconsin

Sue Harings made her first solo canoe trip into the Quetico in October, 1990. Since then, she has paddled a remote Canadian river every year. Many of Susie's trips last two to three weeks. She is the inventor of the clever "Susie bug net" described in Chapter 11.

"Sitting on wet ground or a damp log is no fun. You'll be much more comfortable if you bring a camp stool. I've tried all types and a simple folding model with a canvas seat is best. The stool must have horizontal legs that won't dig into soft ground. My husband, Cliff Jacobson, uses a bungee cord and pair of carabiners to secure his stool to the front of a pack—a fast, effective method. I hand-carry my stool (it weighs almost nothing) or wear it like a necklace on portages.

"Your feet will suffer if you have many tough portages and wear the same boots every day. I bring two different styles of shoes for portaging. When my feet begin to hurt, I switch shoes. For example: I may wear knee-high rubber boots one day and tennis shoes and Tingley rubber overshoes the next day. I wear the tennies alone in camp, or I go barefoot.

"Bring a small space blanket to use as 'outdoor carpeting' at the doorway of your tent. After a swim, I stand on the space blanket to change clothes. In the morning, I pull all my gear out of the tent and pack it on the space blanket. I keep the space blanket in my tent (and out of the weather) until it is needed.

"Things may be forgotten on portages if you don't have a good way to account for them. I stack all my gear in one place at the end of a portage. As an added measure, I tie bright colored plastic flagging (surveying ribbon) to my pack, camera, binoculars, and carbon-black Zaveral canoe paddle.

"Always carry *your own* gear on portages. That way you won't forget anything. If you carry someone else's gear, *tell them* before you carry it. This will ensure that no one retraces a portage to look for something that is already on the other side!"

Jeff Destross

Jeff Destross discovered the Boundary Waters in 1981, when he was a student in Cliff Jacobson's ninth-grade environmental science class. Since 1987 he has organized and led annual canoe trips for teenagers and adults. Jeff cares deeply about young people and the environment. Those who have traveled with Jeff say that he has the cleanest campsites in the Boundary Waters.

"On the water early, off the water early—that's the key to a relaxing Boundary Waters experience. Few things are more frustrating than searching for an unoccupied campsite along a popular route when it's late in the day and you're tired from paddling and portaging.

"Resist the temptation to cook a big breakfast on days when you'll be traveling very far. Save slow-cooking pancakes and fish for mornings when you plan to stay in the same site for another day. Granola bars, pop tarts, and jerky make a fast, nutritious breakfast. Save big meals for camp when you can relax and enjoy the food. I'm usually up at 5:30, and on the water by 6:00. Early morning is a delightful time to paddle: The air is cool, the rising fog is glorious, the water is like glass, and dripping paddles are the only sounds you hear. Five hours of canoeing is enough for me. I'm usually camped by noon and have the rest of the day to swim and relax. Start early, stop by noon, and you'll have your pick of the choice campsites."

Jim Dale Huot-Vickery

Jim has canoed throughout Quetico and the BWCA. He is the author of *Wilderness Visionaries: Open Spaces, Winter Sign*, and is writing a book called *Quest—Sea*, the tale of his thousand-mile 1996 canoe journey from northeastern Minnesota to Hudson Bay, following the Boundary Waters to the sea.

"Go slow. Take your time! Think long-term endurance, not frantic speed. It's just as important to absorb where you are as to get where you think you're going. Pay attention to the 'sonic' wilderness, the sounds and the silence. Feel the wind. Drink big gulps of sky and clouds.

"Feast your eyes on the beauty.

"Consider, in this regard, establishing a layover base camp once in a while. Stay for a full day at least, and spend it resting, looking, listening—letting the land, sky, and water sink in. Fix things. Write in a journal. Experiment and improvise. Ponder or practice love. Perform a random act of kindness for someone. Without breaking camp, explore a lake's entire shoreline. Poke into bays.

"Drift and talk.

"Drift and dream.

"Scout.

"Then, when ready, return to camp. No rush. No competition with other canoeists to score a campsite. Nothing to do but arrive and embrace the night like a friend knocking gently at the door."

Advice from an Outfitter— Marti and Bob Marchino

Marti and Bob Marchino operate Clearwater Canoe Outfitters and Lodge. They are "a small outfitter by choice." Located at the edge of the Boundary Waters, they are the only outfitter on 7-mile-long Clearwater Lake. Marti and Bob paddle the BWCA and Quetico Park yearly to test new

equipment, explore routes, and enjoy their home in the woods. They can be reached at (800) 527–0554 or paddle@canoebwca.com.

"Packing is a science and everything has its place. When we (your outfitter) packed your gear before your canoe trip, we used every inch of pack space. If you don't put things back the same way, they may not fit. For this reason, we advise our customers to use their journal to record how the gear and food were packed by their outfitter. This is easily done as you unpack at your first campsite. After a few days, you'll have the method down pat and will no longer need your notes.

"When portaging, save your back and use a two-person pickup. While one person elevates the bow of the canoe, the other person can walk under, get it balanced, and carry it through the portage." [Author's note: This method is energy efficient, but as noted in Chapter 7, it may damage the ends of your canoe.]

"When carrying the canoe, occasionally lift one shoulder higher than the other. Alternate each shoulder as you walk. This has a relaxing and refreshing effect.

"Use your left or right arm to alternately lift the canoe several inches above your shoulder every so often to avoid stress on your shoulders. Periodically switch to the opposite side.

"Drop your arm occasionally to let the blood circulate and refresh your shoulder and arms."

Appendix I

Equipment Checklist

Many experienced Boundary Waters paddlers use an equipment checklist similar to the one below. They lay out on the floor all their equipment, then they check off items as they are packed. I almost always follow this procedure. On the few trips where I didn't, I have paid dearly. Once, I left behind my tool/repair kit; on another occasion I forgot my L. L. Bean boots and dishwashing materials. Use this checklist as a guide, modify it to suit your needs, then follow it religiously! Space is provided for you to add your favorite items.

People who are new to the Boundary Waters usually bring too much. Some experienced outdoors people sort their gear into three piles—the *essentials*, the *almost essentials*, and the *luxuries*. They take all of the first pile, none of the second, and one luxury item!

Checklist of Gear for a Party of Two People for One Week

Group Equipment

- Four-person tent (7 x 9 feet), preferably with self-supporting framework
- Plastic ground cloth for use inside the tent
- 10 x 10 foot (or larger) coated nylon rain tarp, with a half dozen stakes and 100 feet of cord to rig it
- Three Duluth packs (#3 size), or two packs and a hard-shelled wanigan box or pack basket
- Waterproof plastic liners for the Duluth packs
- 50 feet of ¼-inch-diameter nylon rope
- Folding saw
- Hand axe
- Repair and tool kit: "Leatherman," "Gerber multi-pliers," or similar multipurpose tool; instant epoxy; repair kit for eyeglasses; needle and thread;

buttons; copper rivets; duct tape; file; sharpening stone
- Sponge for cleaning the canoe
- Fillet knife or sheath knife
- Pocketknife
- Cook kit, teakettle or coffee pot, silverware
- Dishwashing materials: 3M nylon scratcher, small bottle of biodegradable detergent, absorbent synthetic "pack towel" for dish drying
- Graduated two-quart plastic shaker, for bailing the canoe and mixing instant drink mixes
- Stove and gasoline; allow two liters of gasoline per week for a party of two.
- Cigarette lighter and matches in waterproof containers
- Fire Ribbon or other emergency chemical fire-starting material
- Small pocket thermometer to settle temperature arguments
- One large candle to aid in starting fires
- First-aid kit in waterproof container

Individual Equipment
- Life jacket
- Two paddles: one lightweight for lakes, one heavyweight for rocky shallows
- Sleeping bag and foam pad
- One long-sleeved wool shirt
- Two cotton T-shirts
- One tightly woven, insect-resistant, long-sleeved cotton-polyester shirt
- One medium-weight wool, pile, or acrylic sweater
- One pair lightweight polyester, wool, or polypropylene two-piece long johns
- One ultralight nylon wind shell (not waterproof). Rolls to fist size
- Four pairs heavy wool socks
- Four pairs lightweight wool, polypropylene, or polyester "liner" socks
- Two pairs long trousers—army fatigues are ideal. *Don't bring blue jeans*!
- Lightweight nylon bathing suit
- Light nylon shorts for blistering hot days
- Cotton web belt—dries faster than leather
- Three changes of underwear
- Toiletries: Biodegradable soap, toothbrush, comb, small towel, etc.
- Chapstick and hand lotion

- Two large cotton bandannas
- One pair of comfortable running shoes for camp use
- One pair of sturdy 6- to 10-inch-high boots for portaging
- Light pair of gloves for cold days—acrylic gloves with "rubber dots" are ideal.
- Small flashlight
- Map set in waterproof case
- Extra map
- Insect repellent
- Compact head net
- Two-piece rain suit
- A brimmed hat for sun (with chin strap) and a wool stocking cap for chilly days. A fully waterproof hat is useful.
- Extra glasses if you wear them
- Sunglasses
- Security strap for glasses
- Camera and film, plus waterproof camera bag
- Compact binoculars for viewing wildlife
- Compact fishing gear (Three Mepps spinners, three Rapalas, three Daredevles, two jigs, and a silver spoon are enough. Store rods in protective plastic cases when paddling and portaging. Put your reel in an old sock and set it at the top of your pack, just under the closing flap.)
- Journal, pencil, paperback book for rainy days.
- _____
- _____
- _____
- _____
- _____
- _____
- _____

Appendix 2

Resources

BWCA Information and Permits

BWCAW Reservation Service
P.O. Box 462
Ballston, NY 12020
Phone: (877) 550–6777 (toll free)
Fax: (518) 884–9951
TDD: (877) TDD-NRRS (toll free)
Web site: www.bwcaw.org
All permits go through the BWCAW Reservation Service in Ballston, New York.

Superior National Forest, Forest Supervisor
8901 Grand Avenue Place
Duluth, MN 55808-1102
Phone (218) 626–4300
TTY: (218) 626–4399
Web site (information only):
www.fs.fed.us/r9/superior
Contact Superior National Forest for canoeing and camping information.

Superior National Forest District Office, Gunflint Ranger District
P.O. Box 790
Grand Marais, MN 55808
Phone and TTY: (218) 387–1750

Superior National Forest District Office, Kawishiwi Ranger District
118 S. 4th Avenue East
Ely, MN 55731
Phone: (218) 365–7600
TTY: (218) 365–7692

Superior National Forest District Office, LaCroix Ranger District
320 North Highway 53
Cooke, MN 55723
Phone: (218) 666–0020
TTY: (218) 666–0021

Superior National Forest District Office, Laurentian Ranger District
318 Forest Road
Aurora, MN 55705
Phone: (218) 229–8800
TTY: (218) 229–3371

Superior National Forest District Office, Tofte Ranger District
Box 2159
Tofte, MN 55615
Phone: (218) 663–8060
TTY: (218) 663–7280

Superior National Forest District
Office, Isabella Work Station
759 Highway 1
Isabella, MN 55607
Phone and TTY: (218) 323–7722

Quetico Information and Permits

Quetico Provincial Park
District Manager
Ministry of Natural Resources
108 Saturn Avenue
Atikokan, Ontario
Canada P0T 1C0
Phone (U.S. residents): (807) 597–2735
Phone (Canadian residents): (807)
597–273a7
To reserve a permit for a canoe trip:
(888) ONT-PARK
Questions about canoeing in Quetico:
(807) 597–2735
To hear a recorded message about cur-
rent Quetico park conditions: (807)
597–4602.
Quetico web site:
www.mnr.gov.on.ca/MNR/parks
Ontario Parks web site: www.ontari-
oparks.com

Customs

U.S. Customs
Phone: (218) 720–5201
Canada Customs
Revenue Canada, Customs and Excise
210-33 Court Street South
Thunder Bay, Ontario
Canada P7B 2W6
Phone: (807) 964–2095
For those driving to Quetico via
Thunder Bay or entering at the

Cache Bay Ranger Station
or
Canada Customs
Revenue Canada, Customs and Excise
301 Scott Street
Fort Frances, Ontario
Canada P9A 1H1
Phone: (807) 274–9780
For those driving to Quetico via Fort
Francis, planning to fly to Atikokan,
or entering at the Lac La Croix or
Prairie Portage Ranger Stations
*Note: You will need a Remote Area
Border Crossing Permit, available
from Canada Customs, if you enter
Canada at the Cache Bay or Prairie
Portage Ranger Stations during the
off season, when the ranger stations
are closed. Pre-clearance to Canada
must be arranged at least six weeks
in advance of your trip.*

Minnesota Licenses

Minnesota Department of Natural
Resources
Box 40, 500 Lafayette Square
Street Paul, MN 55146
(800) 285–2000
For hunting, fishing, and trapping
information. Fishing licenses are
available by mail from the
Department of Natural Resources.

Minnesota Department of Natural
Resources
License Bureau
500 Lafayette Square
Street Paul, MN 55146
Phone: (800) 285–2000
Watercraft in Minnesota must be

licensed unless they are currently licensed in another state. Licenses cost $14.00 for three years and are available by mail from the Department of Natural Resources office in Lafayette Square. Having an unlicensed canoe is a misdemeanor in Minnesota and is subject to a fine of $10 to $700.

Organizations

Friends of the Boundary Waters Wilderness

1313 Fifth Street SE, Suite 329
Minneapolis, MN 55414
(612) 379–3835

"The Friends," as they are known, are the leading environmental watch-dogs for the BWCA and Quetico Provincial Park. They produce a quar-terly newsletter, which keeps mem-bers abreast of environmental con-cerns. They also sponsor the produc-tion of BWCA-specific environmental education materials for schools and nature centers. Membership is $25 per year. The organization's director, Kevin Proescholdt, is a serious envi-ronmental activist whose thought-provoking articles regularly appear in national magazines.

Lake States Interpretive Association

HCR9, Box 600
International Falls, MN 56649
Phone: (218) 283–2103

Lake States Interpretive Association is a non-profit organization that sup-ports the publication and sales of educational materials to visitors to the areas it serves. Request their free catalog of BWCA and Superior National Forest related maps, books, and recreation guides.

BWCA Wilderness Education Consortium

1313 5th Street SE, Suite 329
Minneapolis, MN 55414
(612) 379–3835

Source of two quality videos that describe low impact camping tech-niques for the Boundary Waters Canoe Area. Michael Tezla, an actor with the Guthrie Theater in Minneapolis portrays the experienced camper in the twenty-one-minute version of Leave No Trace—A Wilderness Ethic. A shorter, six-minute version of the video is also available. The videos are very inex-pensive.

Information on Resorts and Outfitters

Cook Chamber of Commerce

P.O. Box 59
Cook, MN 55723
Phone: (800) 648–5897

Crane Lake Commercial Club

Crane Lake, MN 55725
Phone: (800) 362–7405

Ely Chamber of Commerce

1660 East Sheridan Street
Ely, MN 55731
Phone: (218) 365–6123

Lutsen-Tofte Tourism Association
Box 2248
Tofte, MN 55615
Phone: (218) 663–7804

Tip of the Arrowhead Association
Grand Marais, MN 55604
Phone: (800) 622–4014 or (218) 387–2524

Maps

McKenzie Map Company
315 West Michigan Street, Suite 10
Duluth, MN 55802
Phone: (800) 749–2113
Drawn on a scale of 2 inches to the mile (1:31,680), McKenzie maps are beautifully printed on nearly inde-structible Polyart 2 or Tyvek paper. McKenzie maps have crisp contour lines, specified contour intervals, and accurate declination diagrams that show the difference between true and magnetic north. Contact McKenzie for a free index to maps of the BWCA and Quetico Provincial Park.

W. A. Fisher Company
P.O. Box 1107
Virginia, MN 55792
W. A. Fisher Company maps are printed on waterproof paper and are reproduced in a variety of scales from ⅓ inch to the mile to 2½ inches to the mile. Contour intervals and declination information are not spec-ified. Large scale hydrographic maps of the most popular fishing lakes are available.

U.S. Geological Survey Map Sales
P.O. Box 25286, Federal Center, Bldg. 810
Denver, Colorado 80225
Phone: (888) ASK-USGS
Request a free Index to Minnesota topographic maps. USGS maps do not indicate the location of portages, campsites, or hiking trails. You can phone in your order and charge maps to a credit card. All USGS maps have GPS compatible coordinates.

Canada Map Office
615 Booth Street
Ottawa, Ontario
Canada K1AOE9
Phone: (800) 465–6277
Request free Index #1, which covers Ontario and Quetico Provincial Park. Until 1997, you could order Canadian topographic maps from the Canada Map Office. Now you must get them from a U.S. or Canadian map distributor. Call the Canada Map Office for a list of dis-tributors.

Miscellaneous Equipment and Supplies

Bushwacker Backpack and Supply Co.
Missoula, Montana
Phone: (406) 728–6241
A mail-order source of "Counter Assault," a powerful pepper spray that discourages determined bears without hurting them. Expensive but worth it. Large and small versions are available. The large, one-pound can has an effective range of about 10

yards, plus enough product to sustain several long bursts. Designed for use on animals (an illustrated bear is pictured on the label), it is one of the few "Mace-like" products that is legal in Canada. Order the handy holster or tape a snap clip to the can.

Caldwell Outdoor Enterprises
1335 West 11th
Port Angeles, WA 98362
Phone: (206) 457–3009
    A mail-order source of the highly acclaimed "Counter Assault" bear repellent and "quick-draw" holsters.

Chosen Valley Canoe Accessories
P.O. Box 474
Chatfield, MN 55923
Phone: (507) 867–3961
E-mail: k2carr@aol.com
    Source for the slick removable pot handles I inspired. They also have a high-tech yoke that works well on lightweight canoes.

Gransfors Bruks, Inc.
821 West 5th North Street
P.O. Box 818
Summerville, SC 29483
Phone: (800) 433–2863
Fax: (803) 821–2285
    Absolutely the best axes on the planet. Hand forged, superbly balanced, and razor sharp.

Nationwide Marketing, Inc.
1550 Bryant Street, Suite 850
San Francisco, CA 94103
Phone: (800) 777–5452

Source for the Tilia Foodsaver, which I use to vacuum-seal many of my camping foods to retard spoilage.

Cabela's, Inc.
812-13th Avenue
Sidney, NB 69160
Phone: (800) 237–4444
Another source for the Tilia Foodsaver.

The Original Bug Shirt
908 Niagara Falls Boulevard #467
    North Tonawanda, NY 14120
    or
Box 127
Trout Creek, Ontario
Canada P0H 2L0
Phone: (800) 998–9096
    E-mail: bugshirt@onlink.net
    Body armor that stops bugs cold! Proven in the Boundary Waters and beyond.

Recovery Engineering, Inc.
2229 Edgewood Avenue South
Minneapolis, MN 55426
    Manufacturer of PUR water filtration devices. I heartily recommend the PUR Explorer, Scout, and Hiker.

Viking Safety Products
710 Raymond Avenue
Street Paul, MN 55114
Phone: (800) 328–6505 or (612) 646–6374
    Source of sturdy, low-cost, industrial-grade rain gear, plastic Duluth pack liners, and wonderful "Tingley" rubber over-shoes.

Packsacks, Map Cases, and Other Canoeing Luggage

Camp Trails
P.O. Box 966
Binghamton, NY 13902
Phone: (607) 779–2200

A division of Johnson Camping, Camp Trails manufactures state-of-the-art backpacks and accessories.

Cooke Custom Sewing
7290 Stagecoach Trail
Lino Lakes, MN 55014-1988
Phone: (612) 784–8777

Cooke Custom Sewing equipment is designed by serious outdoors people for use by serious outdoors people. Dan Cooke manufactures the canoe splash covers I designed; these are described in my book, *Canoeing Wild Rivers*. Cooke also makes outstanding packs, rain tarps, canoeing accessories, and the "Susie Bug Net," designed by my wife, Sue Harings.

Duluth Pack
P.O. Box 16024
Duluth, MN 55816-0024
Phone: (800) 777–4439
Fax: (218) 722–9575
Catalog sales: Duluth Pack Store, (800) 849–4489

Home of the original Duluth pack, which was designed in 1911 by Camille Porier. These warm and wonderful packs are still made the old-fashioned way from the best water-repellent canvas, top grain leather, and solid copper rivets. Call for their free catalog, which contains dozens of great items.

Grade VI Ltd.
P.O. Box 8
Urbana, IL 61801-0008
Phone: (217) 328–6666 or (612) 222–2917

Charlie Wilson's Grade VI equipment is internationally known. Well designed, incredibly tough, and one of the best map cases around.

Granite Gear
Industrial Park, P.O. Box 278
Two Harbors, MN 55616
Phone: (218) 834–6157

Superior grade nylon canoe packs, thwart bags, and paddling gear.

L. L. Bean, Inc.
Freeport, ME 04033
Phone: (800) 221–4221

Is there anyone who hasn't heard of L. L. Bean? Great store, super catalog, and one of the few mail-order sources for woven ash pack baskets.

Ostrom Outdoors
RR #1, Nolalu
Ontario
Canada P0T 2K0
Phone: (807) 473–4499

Superbly designed high-tech packs and paddling accessories for those who demand the best. Bill Ostrom makes good stuff!

Piragis Northwoods Company
105 North Central Avenue
Ely, MN 55731
Phone: (800) 223-6565
Web site: www.piragis.com
E-mail: info@piragis.com
   A huge and wonderful canoeing and camping store! America's largest We-no-nah canoe dealer, and a source of everything you need for canoeing the Boundary Waters and beyond. Great catalog, good deals. Nice people.

Quetico Superior Canoe Packs
A Division of CLG Enterprises
P.O. Box 6687
Minneapolis, MN 55406
Phone: (800) 328-5215
   Superior Canoe Packs is a division of CLG Enterprises—an internationally known firm that specializes in the manufacture of state-of-the-art outdoor gear. Superior packs feature the finest nickel-plated hardware and top-grain leather. The company carries heavy duty (6 mil) plastic bags for Duluth packs, and manufactures the excellent Hard Pack recommended in Chapter 8. The insulated "Cliff cozy," recommended in Chapter 9, is a hot new item.

Stormy Bay Enterprises
P.O. Box 345
Grand Rapids, MN 55744
   Manufacturers of the excellent "Wanigan Canoe Pack & Pantry" described in Chapter 8.

Zaveral Racing Equipment, Inc.
242 Lockwood Hill Road
Mt. Upton, NY 13809
Phone: (607) 563-2487
Web site: www.zre.com
E-mail: zaveralb@zre.com
   In my opinion, the best graphite canoe paddles on the planet. Zaveral paddles are also available from We-no-nah Canoe Company.

BWCA and Quetico Canoeing Guide Books

   A Paddler's Guide to the Boundary Waters Canoe Area in Northeastern Minnesota, by Michael Duncanson. 76 pp., softcover. Provides detailed descriptions of thirty-one wilderness canoe routes. Includes twelve updated canoeing maps. Available from W. A. Fisher Company.
   Paddler's Guide to Quetico Provincial Park, by Robert Beymer. 168 pp., softcover. A guide to eighteen entry points and thirty-one routes. Includes campsite locations, portages, and location of pictographs. Four-color fold-out map. Available from W. A. Fisher Company.

Appendix 3
Seven-Day Menu

Day 1

Breakfast: Canadian bacon, fresh eggs as you like 'em, steamed raisin bagels, Tang, coffee

Lunch: pita bread, peanut butter and jam (PBJ), hard salami, cookies, instant drink mix

Supper: stir-fry steak, fresh onions, green peppers, and tomatoes over rice; lettuce and tomato salad, Cup-a-Soup

Day 2

Breakfast: cheese omelet, Canadian bacon, steamed English muffin with margarine and jam, Tang, coffee

Lunch: pita bread, PBJ, beef jerky, half an apple, salted nut roll, instant drink mix

Supper: smoked bratwursts on the grill, pita bread buns with mustard, Ramen noodle soup

Day 3

Breakfast: cinnamon-sugar rice and golden raisins, stewed mixed evaporated fruit, Tang, coffee

Lunch: seasoned Rye Krisp, Swiss cheese, carrots, PBJ, "soft batch" chocolate chip cookies, instant drink mix

Supper: hamburger/cheese/vegetable soup with noodles, fresh onion, and carrots; dark chocolate bar

Day 4

Breakfast: Big Bill's Multi Grain Cereal with raisins, dehydrated apples, crushed walnuts, and brown sugar; Tang; coffee

Lunch: pita bread, PBJ, hard salami, mixed nuts, instant drink mix

Supper: spaghetti made with dehydrated hamburger, tomato powder, fresh onion; Cup-a-Soup, M & M candies

Day 5

Breakfast:	Red River Cereal with raisins, dates, crushed walnuts, and brown sugar; Tang; coffee
Lunch:	sesame-flavored Rye Krisp, fresh provolone cheese, beef jerky, PBJ, fresh carrots, macaroon cookies, instant drink mix
Supper:	pita pizza, chicken noodle soup, fresh red cabbage and onion salad

Day 6

Breakfast:	multigrain pancakes, fried hard salami, Tang, coffee
Lunch:	pita bread, PBJ, Monterey jack cheese, GORP, instant drink mix
Supper:	chili made with dehydrated hamburger and beans, with macaroni and onion added

Day 7

Breakfast:	cinnamon-sugar tortillas and stewed fruit, Tang, coffee
Lunch:	flavored Rye Krisp, fresh dill cheese, PBJ, M & M peanut candy, instant drink mix
Dinner:	grilled garlic-cheese pita melt, Ramen noodles with dehydrated hamburger, fresh onion and carrots

Appendix 4
The Wilderness Meal—
A Backcountry Ethics Learning Activity

Please read chapter 5 before doing this activity.

Here's a non-intimidating way to teach low impact camping procedures to anyone who is about to experience a Boundary Waters adventure. This activity is structured for Junior High School students but it has been successfully used—and enthusiastically received—by thousands of adults. It's a natural for schools, scouts, summer camps, and nature centers.

You'll need 2-3 hours to prepare students for the activity and pack the food. "Prep time" may be broken into convenient time blocks that suit your schedule. At least 80 minutes of uninterrupted time will be needed for the actual cook-out. Bad weather spoils student attitudes, so reschedule the event if it rains.

Overview of the Activity

Students build a "no trace" campfire and cook a simple meal that has no bottles or cans to pollute the environment. A "Forest Ranger" (the class instructor) visits the group and quizzes them on the twelve minimum impact rules of their BOUNDARY WATERS WILDERNESS PERMIT (see **Figure A-2**). Students lose points for environmentally incorrect answers and/or not knowing the *rationale* for each rule. After the cook-out, students clean up the fire site and restore the area to pristine condition. The "Ranger" returns, checks for human sign, then awards or deducts points, as necessary.

Where to do the Activity

A wooded setting is best but an outdoor hockey rink, track or graveled school yard works fine. Students "leave no trace" of their activity so there is no damage to the environment. My eighth grade environmental science students have built more than 500 fires in a school hockey rink over the last fifteen years, and school administrators can't find one of them!

Materials Needed, Per Group of Four

1. One three pound coffee can (free from your school cafeteria), fitted with a wire bail made from a coat hanger.
2. Three plastic bags and rubber bands to seal them
3. A one gallon water container (a clean plastic milk jug is ideal).
4. A sharp pocket knife and small trowel (or substitute an aluminum tube with one end flattened).
5. The instructor furnishes strike anywhere matches.
6. Individual eating utensils—plastic cup, plastic bowl, metal spoon.

Unit Timing

Introduction

1. Begin by telling the students that the "Wilderness Meal" activity simulates a real Boundary Waters experience. Give a brief historical view of the BWCA (see chapter 1) and explain the importance of "low impact" camping. A 21 minute video, Leave No Trace—A Wilderness Ethic, is available at low cost from the BWCA Wilderness Education Consortium (address in appendix 2). Ask your librarian about other films and film strips that teach wilderness ethics.
2. Explain the role of the group leader. The leader is responsible for seeing to it that everyone knows the rules and the rationale behind them. Each group should appoint a "leader."
3. If the activity is done in an unnatural area where firewood cannot be collected, each group must furnish a paper shopping bag filled with dry wood. Wood should range in size from pencil lead thickness to no larger than what can be broken over the knee. Lumber, birch bark, leaves, paper, pine needles and other unnatural materials may not be used!

Discuss the Wilderness Permit (40 minutes)

Hand out one copy of the BOUNDARY WATERS WILDERNESS PERMIT (**Figure A-2**) to each group of four people. Read and explain the rationale behind each of the rules. Be prepared for a flood of questions. You may want to review chapters 5, 10 and 12 before you introduce this activity.

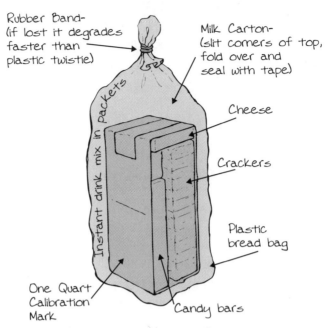

Labels on figure:
Rubber Band- (if lost it degrades faster than plastic twistie)

Milk Carton- (slit corners of top, fold over and seal with tape)

Instant drink mix in Packets

Cheese

Crackers

Plastic bread bag

One Quart Calibration Mark

Candy bars

Figure A-1. Packing up The Wilderness Meal.

Discuss Low-Impact Foods (40 minutes)

1. Explain why a "wilderness meal" should be compact, lightweight, waterproof, easy and fast to prepare, and contain no cans or bottles to pollute the environment. Discuss foods that are suitable for a BWCA experience (review chapter 9).

2. The Meal: Groups of 3-4 students will prepare a simple stew from the ingredients listed below.

Food Items

- Any favorite instant soup mix. Adjust the amounts based on servings per package.
- One cup Bisquick™ or other dumpling mix.
- One cup instant rice.
- Choose any number of these or similar items: Crackers, fruit roll-ups, beef sticks, beef jerky, salted nut rolls, granola bars, GORP (good old raisins and

peanuts) made with a mixture of M&M's, Cheerios, sunflower seeds, raisins, peanuts, etc., or candy and cookies that will "melt in your mouth, not in your hands."

• Kool-aid'™, Wylers™, Tang'™, or other instant flavored drink mix.

Food Packing Day (40 minutes)!

Students follow these guidelines to package their meal

1. Measure one cup of rice into a plastic bag and seal the bag with a rubber band. Set aside this bag.
2. Measure one cup of Bisquick™ into a plastic bag and seal the bag with a rubber band. Set aside this bag.
3. Remove and discard excess packaging on all remaining food items. Pour dry food out of jars into plastic bags.
4. Place all food into a crush-resistant cardboard milk carton and place the carton inside a plastic bag, as illustrated in figure A-1. Non-crushable foods like "Kool-Aid" that won't fit may be packed between the milk carton and waterproof plastic bag. Students may use the milk carton to mix powdered soft drinks.
5. Label the milk carton or outer plastic bag with the group leader's name. When students have completed packaging their meal, they should perform these tests:

    A) Waterproof test (simulates a canoe capsize): Dunk the meal in a tank of water for 30 seconds.

    B) Shock test: Throw the meal lightly(!) against a wall to simulate the abuse of a week on the trail.
6. The instructor keeps all packed meals in a large trash bag for several days prior to the cook-out. This ensures that "illegal" food items that might spoil or melt will!

Firemaking Day (40-80 minutes)!

1. (20 minutes) Optional: Read aloud the short story, "To Build A Fire," by Jack London. Prior to reading the tale, challenge students to identify the man's greatest mistake. Answer: Instead of building a fire, the man should have brought a change of clothes and a warm sleeping bag. An open fire is not a good survival tool in bitter cold weather.

2. (40-60 minutes) Teach students how to build a "no trace" fire. Procedure: Carefully remove a sixteen inch diameter piece of sod eight inches deep and pile the diggings on top of the inverted sod cap. Build a hot fire in the hole. Students should whittle fine shavings for tinder and use small twigs for kindling.

    If an outside site is not available to demonstrate fire-building, the instructor should build a mock fire on a table or overhead projector.

3. Students should burn only enough wood to cook the meal. The fire must be allowed to burn until all the wood has turned to ashes. The sod cap is replaced and the area is smoothed to blend with the environment. No trace of the fire should remain.

Cookout! (80-100 minutes)

- Students are assigned "campsites." They dig their holes, light their fires and follow this procedure to cook their meal.

1. Read the directions on the soup package. Add 20 percent more water to the tin can pot than is suggested. Pour the soup mix into the cold water and place the pot on the fire.

2. Add some cold water to the bag of dumpling mix and knead the bag with your hands. continue to knead and add water until the dough has a soft clay-like consistency. When the soup in the pot is boiling, cut a slit in the bag bottom and, using the bag like a cake decorator, force marble sized dumplings into the hot soup.

3. Add the instant rice to the boiling soup.

4. Stir the soup constantly for ten minutes using a long stick whose bark has been removed with a pocket knife.

5. Serve and enjoy!

- At some time during the activity, the instructor (camp ranger) comes on the scene. The ranger asks to see the "Wilderness Permit," then questions the students about the rules. Students must know the rationale for every regulation. Points are deducted for wrong answers.
- When clean-up is complete, the ranger returns to check each fire site.

BOUNDARY WATERS WILDERNESS PERMIT

Welcome to the Boundary Waters Canoe Area Wilderness! Thousands of people have fought hard to preserve the wilderness character of this region. We hope you will do your part to keep the BWCA clean, green and free of pollution.

You are required to have this permit with you at all times while in the BWCA. You must show your permit to a Forest Ranger on request. Please fill out the information below:

Name of Group Leader: _____

Number of Members in the Group: _____

(Maximum of nine is permitted)

Date: _____ Number of Days You Will Stay _____
in the Boundary Waters

RULES

1. Camp only at designated campsites. Do not occupy just any site.

2. Build fires in designated areas only. Pack out—*do not burn*, aluminum foil! Put your fires *dead out* (check it with your hand) before you leave! A "dead" fire has no visible smoke or steam! Clean up the fire site so as to *leave no trace of humans*.

3. Absolutely no cans or bottles or materials designed to be "obviously disposable" are allowed. This means no styrofoam cups, plastic silverware or margarine tubs!

4. Use only dead and downed wood for fire building. Go far away from the lakeshore and your campsite to collect firewood.

5. Cutting or marking living trees is strictly prohibited! Do not peel birch bark or remove leaves or branches from living trees.

6. Do not dig a trench around your tent to carry away storm water. Trenching is ugly and it causes serious soil erosion. You'll stay dry in the rain if you place a plastic ground-cloth *inside* your tent.

7. Burn your trash, and *pack out* what won't burn! Be sure you have brought a strong plastic bag for this purpose. Hang your trash bag from a tree limb so you can find it easily. Forest Rangers may ask to see your trash bag!

8. *Be aware of your campsite responsibility.* You are *required* to keep a clean, orderly campsite at all times. If you generate trash, pick it up immediately and put it in your trash bag. If your campsite was trashed by thoughtless persons before you, *you* must clean up their mess!

9. Do not wash dishes, bathe or swim within 150 feet of a lake or river. Dishes—and your body—should be washed (with biodegradable soap) and rinsed on land, well away from water.

10. If nature calls and no official latrine (toilet) is available, go out of the camp area, 150 feet from water, and carefully bury human waste and toilet paper under a 4-6 inch cover of soil.

11. Respect the rights of others! Loud screaming, radios and other disturbing sounds will not be tolerated.

12. Leave your campsite in a natural state. *Do not lash* or nail logs together to make tables, chairs or other furniture. These activities spoil the wilderness experience for the next party who occupies your campsite.

Figure A-2.

Appendix 5
McKenzie Map Index

BWCAW QUETICO
A1. BWCA and Quetico Area Map
A1. Laminated
1. Pine, Greenwood, Mountain
2. E. Bearskin, Clearwater, Alder
3. Ball Club, Winchell, Poplar
4. Gunflint, Loon, North
4A. Gunflint W/ Water Depths
5. Magnetic, Gunflint, Northern L.
6. Saganga, Sea Gull
6A. Saganga, Saganagons
7. Little Saganga, Tuscarora
8. Knife, Kekekabic, Thomas
9. Moose, Basswood, Snowbank
10. Basswood, Crooked, Sarah
10A. Basswood Depth Contour Map
11. Jackfish, Beartrap, Thursday
12. Moose River, Stuart
13. Lac La Croix
14. Loon, Wilkins, Little Indian Sioux
15. Trout
16. Burntside, Cummings
17. Fall, Pipestone
18. Lake One, Bald Eagle
19. Isabella, Insula
20. Alton, Perent
21. Sawbill, Brule, Pipe
22. Arrow, Sandstone
23. Iron Range, Canthook, Jinx
24. Northern Light
25. Saganagons, Mack
26. This Man, Cache
27. Agnes, Kahshahpiwi
28. Brent, Poobah, Conmee
29. Argo, Minn, William
30. Red Pine, Badwater, Snow
31. Lac La Croix, Wolsely, Nam. R.
32. Thompson, David, Namakan R.
33. Beaverhouse, Whalen, Factor
34. Quetico, Cirrus, McCauly
35. Sturgeon, Burntside, Jean
36. Keefer, Williams, Camel
37. Kawnipi

38. Powell, Obadinaw R. Wawiag R.
39. Titmarsh, Plummens, Nelson
40. Burchell
41. Tilly, Windigoostigwan
42. McKenzie, Cache, Buckingham
43. Russel, Olifaunt, Maligne R.
44. Soho, Kasakokwog, Oriana
45. Pickerel, Batchewaung, Nym
46. Pickerel, Eva, Baptism
116. Ely, Shagawa

VOYAGEURS NATIONAL PARK
K1. Kabetogama
N1. Namakan, Sand Point
C1. Crane, Sand Point
R1. Rainy Lake Southwest
R2. Rainy Lake Southeast

ISLE ROYALE
IRE. Isle Royale East
IRC. Isle Royale Central
IRW. Isle Royale West

LAKE SUPERIOR
AI. Apostle Is.
CA. Chequamegon Bay/Apostle. Is.
DS. Duluth/Superior
PC. Port Wing/Cornucopia
TS. Two Harbors/Silver Bay

MN. NORTH SHORE AREA
SUPERIOR NAT'L FOREST
98. Grand Portage
99. Tom Lake
100. Grand Marais
101. Cascade-Bally Creek
102. Lutsen-Tofte
103. Taconite Harbor-Little Marais
104. Beaver Bay-Tettegouche
105. Gooseberry
203. Timber-Frear
204. Dumbell Lake
304. Silver Island

GENERAL MAP INFORMATION

MCKENZIE MAPS of the BWCAW and QUETICO PROVINCIAL PARK are published on a scale of 2"=1 mile. Each map covers an area of approximately 144 square miles. The maps are printed on a 25" x 30" sheet of POLYART plastic paper which is next to indestructible. They are totally waterproof and extremely hard to tear even after folding many times. The maps will easily withstand all the hard use you can give them. They even float!

MCKENZE MAPS can be used for navigation. They contain the most up-to-date information on campsite locations, portages, hiking trails, ski trails, motor regulations, navigation markers where used, topography, and hydrographics.

In addition to a single 25" x 38" souvenir or planning map that covers all of the BWCAW and 90% of QUETICO PARK, there are 25 maps of the BWCAW and 25 QUETICO maps. All

maps are reviewed for accuracy by Park officials, U.S. Forest Service Officials, DNR officials, guides, outfitters, and resort owners.

Sizes of the other maps vary. There are five 25"x 38" maps of VOYAGEURS NATIONAL PARK, three 25" x 38" maps of ISLE ROYALE and APOSTLE IS. NATIONAL LAKESHORE and eleven 25" x 30" or 25" x 38" maps of the Minnesota North Shore of Lake Superior and Superior National Forest. The North Shore maps show the most recent information on Minnesota's popular SUPERIOR HIKING TRAIL.

MCKENZIE MAPS can be purchased at most sporting goods stores, resorts, outfitters, park offices or by calling or writing MCKENZIE PRODUCTS, 315 W. Michigan St., Duluth, MN. 55802, 218–727–2113.

A special thanks to Rod McKenzie for allowing me to use this McKenzie Map Index.

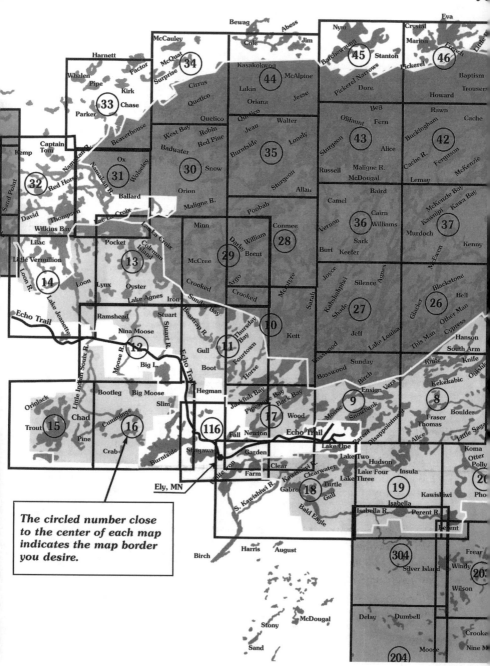

The circled number close to the center of each map indicates the map border you desire.

Boundary Waters Canoe Area
Wilderness, Quetico Provincial Park and
Voyageurs National Park

Maps
By
McKenzie

Distributed By
McKenzie Products

Index

A
address listings, 149-55
adult passenger, paddling, 64-65
ailments, most common, 129-31
aiming off, with mis-plotted feature on map, 28-29
alone, paddling, 64
animals, encountering, 109-12
awakening, to lightning, 122-23
axe, safety with, 125

B
backcountry, ethics learning activity, 159-63
bag, thwart, 51
bear, at campsite, 112-13
big water, paddling, 59-66
black flies, 116-17
blister, on heel, 130-31
boiling, water, 127
bottles, regulations regarding, 41
Boundary Waters, ecological battles, 1-5
breakfasts, 90-92
building materials, canoe, 48-49
burns, lightning, first-aid, 123-24
BWCA and Quetico Canoeing Guide Books, 155
BWCA Reservation Service, address, 149
BWCA Wilderness Education Consortium, address, 151

C
Caldwell Outdoor Enterprises, 153
Camp Trails, 154
campfire
    regulations, 43-44
    unattended, 44
campsite, bear, 112-13
Canada Map Office, 152
Canadian Customs, 150
canoe
    building materials, 48-49
    lightness of, 47
    line, 51
    loading, 59-60
    luggage, 154-55
    outfitting, 49-53
    packing, 85
    paddling, 55-66
    portaging, 66-69
    selecting, 47-53
    speed of, 47-48
    tethering, 124
cans, regulations regarding, 41
carrying yoke, 49-51
cereals, hot, 91
chemicals, water, 127
children, small, carrying, and paddling, 66
cinnamon
    rice with golden raisins, breakfast, 91

tortillas, stewed fruit, Canadian bacon, 92
compass, 24
    using with map, 25-28
containers, for powders/liquids, 90
contour lines, interpretation of, 15-16
Cook Chamber of Commerce, 151
Cooke Custom Sewing, 154
cooking
    pot, 97-99
    tricks, 97
Crane Lake Commercial Club, 151

D
dangers, 121-31
    swimming, 121-22
day-use motor permit, 19
    reserved, 19
declination, magnetic, 24-25
dish washing materials, 90
dislocated shoulder, 130
downwind, running, paddling, 60-62
Duluth Pack, 154

E
ecological concerns, 1-5
eggs, 91-92
    cheese McPita/McTortilla, 91-92
Ely, 10
    Chamber of Commerce, 151
Equipment, 71-85
    checklist, 145-47
    for children, 82-84
    clothing, 80, 82-83
    cooking tarp, 78-79
    cookware, 79-80
    double-packing, 73-74
    edged tools, 80
    entertainment, 84
    footwear, 81-82, 83
    hat, 81
    hip belt, 75-76
    knife, 80
    modern canoe packs, 74-75
    packing, 84-85
    packing canoe, 85
    packs, 72-73
    rain gear, 80-81, 83
    rigid packs, 76-77
    sleeping bags, 82, 83-84
    sleeping gear, 82
    stove, 79-80
    tent, 78
    toys, 84
    tumplines, 72-73
    waterproofing, contents of pack, 77-78
ethics learning activity, 159-63
eye, foreign body in, 129-30

F
filters, for water, 127
fire
    making tips, 107
    regulations, 44
first-aid, 121-31
    kit contents, 128
    mini, 128-29
    lightning burns, 123-24
fish hook, in skin, 129
flies, black, 116-17
folding saw, safety with, 125
foreign body, in eye, 129-30
friction blister, on heel, 130-31
Friends of the Boundary Waters Wilderness, 151
Frost River, 33-35

G
gear, two people for one week, 145-46
Grade IV Ltd., 154
Grand Marais, 10-11
Granite Gear, 154
Granite River through portage, 35-37

H
Ham Lake to Long Island Lake and points east, 31-33
hamburger/cheese vegetable soup, 95
hardware, 88-90
heel, blister on, 130-31
hot cereals, 91
Hubachek, Frank, 2

I
injuries, common, 127-28
insects, 114-16
    repellents, 117-18
Isabella, 10

L
Lake States Interpretive Association, 151
latrine, regulations, 42-43
learning activity, in ethics, 159-63
licensing of canoe, in Minnesota, 19-20
life jackets, 52
lightness, of canoe, 47
lightning, 122
    awakening to, 122-23
    burns, first-aid, 123-24
line, on canoe, 51
liquids, containers for, 90
L.L. Bean, Inc., 154
loading canoe, 59-60
Long Island Lake, from Ham Lake, 31-33
luggage, canoe, 154-55
lunch, 92-93
Lutsen-Tofte Tourism Association, 152

M
McKenzie Map Company, maps, 152
magnetic declination, 24-25
management tricks, 95-96
maps, 11-12, 24

cases, canoeing luggage, 154-55
McKenzie maps, 11
    mis-plotted feature, aiming off, 28-29
    sources of, 152
    using with compass, 25-28
    W.A. Fisher Company maps, 12
McKenzie maps, 11
McPita, 91-92
meals, 87-99
    breakfasts, 90-92
        cinnamon
        rice with golden raisins, 91
        tortillas, stewed fruit, Canadian bacon, 92
    containers, for powders/liquids, 90
    cooking
        pot, 97-99
        tricks, 97
    dish washing materials, 90
    egg, 91-92
    cheese McPita/McTortilla, 91-92
    hamburger/cheese vegetable soup, 95
    hardware, 88-90
    hot cereals, 91
    lunch, 92-93
    management tricks, 95-96
    packing, 90
        in stuff sacks, 96
    pita pizza, 95
    spices, 90
    supper, 93-95
menu, seven-day, 156-57
Minnesota, licensing of canoe in, 19-20
Minnesota Dept. of Natural Resources, address, 150-51
mis-plotted feature on map, aiming off, 28-29
moose trails, navigating, 29

N
no-see-ums, 116, 118-19
number of canoes, regulations, 40-41

O
Olson, Sigurd, 1-2
orienteering compass, 24
outfitters, names and addresses of, 151-52
outfitting canoe, 49-53
    carrying yoke, 49-51
    life jackets, 52
    paddles, 52-53
    sponge, 52
    thwart bag, 51
    small items, 51
overnight permit
    reserved, 19
    walk-in, 19

P
pacing, canoe trip, 7-21
packing, 90
    in stuff sacks, 96
packsacks, 154-55

Paddler's Guide to Quetico Provincial Park, 155
Paddler's Guide to the Boundary Waters Canoe Area in Northeastern Minnesota, 155
paddles, 52-53
paddling, 55-66
  adult passenger, 64-65
  alone, 64
  big water, 59-66
  and carrying small children, 66
  pitch stroke, 55-56
  running upwind and down, 60-62
  on same side, 63
  tacking, 63
  teenage passenger, 64-65
  trim rules, 60
  underwater stroke, 56-58
party size, regulations, 40-41
passenger, canoeing with, 64-65
permits, 18-21
  day-use motor, 19
  reserved day-use motor, 19
  reserved overnight, 19
  walk-in overnight, 19
pita pizza, 95
pitch stroke, paddling, 55-56
pizza, pita, 95
planning, canoe trip, 7-21
portaging canoe, 66-69
powders, containers for, 90

Q
Quetico Provincial Park, 150
  Canada, entry, 20

R
Recovery Engineering, Inc., 153
regulations, 39-45
  bottles, 41
  campfire, 43-44
  unattended, 44
  cans, 41
  latrine, 42-43
  number of canoes, 40-41
  party size, 40-41
  sanitation, 44-45
  U.S. Forest Service, designated sites, 42
  waste disposal, 44-45
  repellent, insect, 117-18
  resorts, names and addresses, 151-52
Robertson, Frank, 3
Route
  favorite, 31-37
  planning, 17
  selection of, 8-11

S
safety, first-aid, 121-31

sanitation, regulations, 44-45
saw, folding, safety with, 125
scenario thought list, 17-18
shoulder, dislocated, 130
side, same, paddling on, 63
skin, fish hook in, 129
small streams, navigating, 29
solitude, favorite routes, 31-37
soup, hamburger/cheese vegetable, 95
speed, of canoe, 47-48
spices, 90
sponge, 52
stingers, 114-16
Stormy Bay Enterprises, 155
supper, 93-95
swimming, dangers, 121-22

T
tacking, 63
teenage passenger, paddling, 64-65
tethering canoe, 124
thwart
  bag, 51
  small item, 51
Tip of the Arrowhead Association, 152
Tofte, 10
tools, safety with, 125
trail meals, 87-99
          see also meals
travel area, selection of, 8-11
treatment procedures, water, 127
tree, wind-downed, 124
trim rules, paddling, 60

U
underwater stroke, paddling, 56-58
upwind, running, paddling, 60-62
U.S. Customs, 150
U.S. Forest Service, designated sites, 42
U.S. Geological Survey Map Sales, 152

V
Viking Safety Products, 153

W
W.A. Fisher Company, maps, 12, 152
waste disposal, regulations, 44-45
water
  boiling, 127
  filters, 127
  quality, 125-27
  treatment chemicals, 127
  treatment procedures, 127
"widow makers," 124
wilderness, ecological concerns, 1-5
wood, dry, 106

Y
yoke, carrying, canoe, 49-51

DULUTH PACK

SINCE 1882

PURVEYORS OF TRADITIONAL NORTHWOODS
PACKS, BAGS AND LUGGAGE.
ORIGINAL MANUFACTURER OF THE
FAMOUS DULUTH PACK SINCE 1911.

CALL FOR OUR FREE CATALOG OF NORTHWOODS GEAR

1-800-777-4439
www.duluthpack.com

Essential vehicles for wilderness travelers

The beauty and peace of the Boundary Waters Canoe Area is matched by its demands on those who travel there. Tough routes. Long portages. Challenging winds and waves that arise quickly and unannounced.

To master this remote land, you need a canoe created to conquer extremes, a craft that will enhance your journey, not encumber it.

We build light, tough, responsive canoes using Kevlar,® Royalex,® or other superior materials. They paddle with grace, portage with ease, and withstand the inevitable abuse. And among our wide selection, several models are designed specifically to master long Boundary Waters trips.

To learn more, visit a dealer, request our informative literature, or see our comprehensive website.

Photos:
Mike Maternowsky
Tom Kaffine

Informative,
40-page
magazine

CANOE
We·no·nah

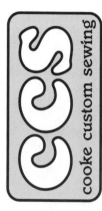

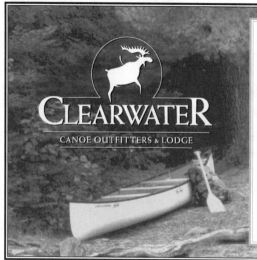

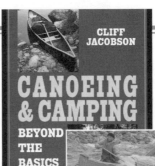